CASSADAGA

Where Spirits Meet

120th Anniversary Edition

Marilyn J. Awtry

DEDICATED TO

The Founder of Cassadaga, Florida

George Prescott Colby

and

The 13 Founders of Southern Cassadaga Spiritualist Camp Meeting Association

Thomas Skidmore - Lily Dale, NY

Marion Skidmore - Lily Dale, NY

Abby L. Pettengill - Cleveland, OH & Lily Dale, NY

Emma J. Huff - Lake Helen, FL & Lily Dale, NY

Frank Bond - Deland, FL

Harvey W. Richardson - East Aurora, NY

Aldailla C. Jewett - Cleveland, OH

Jerry Robinson - Lookout Mountain, TN

Mariette Cuscaden - Tampa, FL

Soledad B. Sofford - Tarpon Springs, FL

George W. Liston - Forest City, FL

George Webster - Lake Helen, FL

Maria H. Webster - Lake Helen, FL

ACKNOWLEDGMENT

My sincere gratitude is extended to Rev. Dr. Louis Gates of Cassadaga, Florida who shared with us his picture album of Post Cards of Cassadaga and Lake Helen, Florida of Yesteryear

http://cassadagacamp.org/v-web/gallery/album02

My sincere gratitude is extended to Rev. Elizabeth (Janie) Owens of Cassadaga for sharing her photographs of the Cassadaga Hotel.

BOOKS BY THE AUTHOR

River of Life: How to Live in the Flow
Seventy-six Spiritual Natural Laws.

Living in the Light: A Guide to Spiritualism's Philosophy
A review of the philosophical aspect of Modern Spiritualism.

Spiritualism and the Bible Connection
Clarifies Spiritualism's understanding
and teachings of the Holy Bible.

Spiritualism on the Move: A Reality
Check for the New Century
Chronological events of the first three 50-year cycles of Modern
Spiritualism and suggestions to sustain itself in the 21st Century.

Light from Beyond the Tomb: Spiritualism Survived
Presentation of original and factual documentation
of the Fox Sisters and Spiritualism.

Path of Light Volume I
Flow of events establishing the foundation of Modern
Spiritualism and its evolution into an organized Science,
Philosophy and Religion for all Spiritualists.

Path of Light Volume II
The Trinity of Spiritualism – the Science, Philosophy
and Religion of Modern Spiritualism leading into the
understanding of Spiritualism as a way of life.

WEBSITE: MARILYNJAWTRY.COM
"Thoughts to Ponder" and "Sunflower Seeds"
are updated monthly.

FOREWORD

I had the pleasure of speaking before the Volusia County Historical Association and received encouragement from several of its members, so the dust-laden manuscript was taken off the shelf, updated and made available for those who wanted the "facts" and not "just another story."

Every narrative has a beginning. The Cassadaga story would not be complete without establishing the firm foundation of the evolution of Modern Spiritualism and the part played by Lake Helen, Florida in its growth and development of the community that became known as Cassadaga, Florida.

Dr. William Rowley is credited with founding the first Spiritualist Camp in Florida at De Leon Springs and naming it the National Spiritual and Liberal Association (NSALA). George P. Colby became its first President. Once the Camp had outgrown its property Abbie Pettengill, Marion and Thomas Skidmore and Emma Huff, all of the City of Light in New York (now the Lily Dale Assembly), were in full agreement with most of the membership to find it a new home. The Cassadaga community so much resembled the northern camp that the group of 13 are credited with having incorporated the Southern Cassadaga Spiritualist Camp Meeting Association (SCSCMA) as a sister Camp to their northern camp.

This unique community of lakes, hills and tall pines became known around the world as the Cassadaga Spiritualist Camp. Credit is given to George P. Colby for homesteading acreage in Lake Helen, Florida and naming it Cassadaga. He deeded a portion of his land to the newly incorporated Southern Cassadaga Spiritualist Camp Meeting Association to be used as a right-of-way for an entrance to the Camp.

The dedication of these pioneers created a sacred place where, over the years many have come seeking help from the unseen side of life. They often came discouraged and without hope. They left with peace within and knowing there was a new path for their life.

This narrative of the "facts" of this evolving community offers a sense of peace mixed with excitement as you travel through the pages of time from 1848 to 2014.

Marilyn J. Awtry
August 2014

Contents

PART I

I

The Symbol of Spiritualism

The Sunflower is the symbol of Modern Spiritualism. It can be traced back to the Ancients who regarded bright yellow as the emblem of Truth and Constancy. In 1887 the American Woman Suffrage Society adopted yellow, the color of sunflower petals as their distinguished badge. They felt that "the sunflower seemed appropriate since it always turns its face to the light and the course of the sun seemingly worshipping the {arche} type of righteousness." In 1892, the Association of Spiritualists at the Cassadaga Lake Free Assembly in Cassadaga, New York first adopted the Sunflower as its official seal.

In the early 1900s, William H. Bach became the second well-known Spiritualist to manufacture Sunflower jewelry. He changed the design of the pin and added brooches and watch fobs.

In 1928, the Sunflower was adopted as the Official Badge of International Spiritualism at the Conference of the International Spiritualist Federation (ISF). In that same time frame, Mrs. Grace Linn Sandy of Indianapolis, Indiana composed the first song entitled *The Sunflower.* In 1928, it was adopted by the National Spiritualist Association (NSA) as their organization's song. In 1983, a second song was composed by Linda N. Alden of Rochester, New York entitled *Like the Sunflowers.*

What was the reasoning behind selecting the Sunflower? Besides its color, it was selected because

- It is native to the soil of our country and it has been known to be transplanted to many other soils around the world.

- Like a magnet it attracts, but it does so selectively. Spiritualism also selectively attracts the individual who is seeking truth.

- It rests upon a strong stalk just as Spiritualism depends upon a strong character.

- Its long reach protects and shields the weaker plants. In the same light, Spiritualism protects humanity from superstitions that prohibit spiritual growth.

✧ It also provides a medicinal value as it contains a complete balance of all natural vitamins and minerals. In comparison, the Philosophy of Spiritualism stresses the balancing of the spiritual, mental and physical being.

The motto supporting the selection of the Sunflower is:

> "As the Sunflower turns its
> Face to the Light of the Sun
> So Spiritualism turns the
> Face of Humanity to the
> Light of Truth."

It is no coincidence that as we entered into the 21st Century, the Age of Aquarius, we began to witness an increase in awareness and spirituality. An understanding of the value of Spiritualism's philosophy justifies the resurgence of the Sunflower as a popular symbol today. It is once again available in gift shops around the world.

II

Before Cassadaga

Mother Ann Lee and the Shakers

Just who was this lady? Ann Lee was born in Manchester, England on February 29, 1736. She faced a life of poverty and at a very young age commenced working long hours in a factory. In 1758 she joined with a Shaker family, James and Jane Wardley. Ann showed signs of prophetic leadership very quickly. She drew others to herself like a magnet. Mother Ann described her many, many visions to her followers.

In 1762, she married Abraham Standerin, a blacksmith, and bore four children in rapid succession. All four died in infancy. As her unhappy marriage came to an end, her life changed drastically. In 1774, she brought the Shaker sect from England to the shores of America and settled in Watervliet, near Albany, New York. She became known as a trailblazer. Her motto was, "Put your hands to work and your hearts to God."

Her expanding group was extremely spiritual and the most successful communal society in the United States. The Shakers were industrious and invented many items such as the circular saw, the clothespin, the broom and a unique style of furniture. The Shakers were recognized for their simplicity, humility, order, peace and simple goodness. They practiced equality of race and sex as well as chastity. Their basic tenets were communal life, confession of sin and celibacy. The question that comes to mind is how they could keep the movement alive? They simply adopted children. At age 21, they were given the opportunity to live outside the commune. After one year, they made the choice as to whether to remain within the Shaker community or go their way into the world.

During the early 1800s, communication with the unseen was not an uncommon practice within communities of Shakers in America. They were known to entertain trance speakers offering communication in unknown tongues from the higher spheres of the Spirit World. Those in the Spirit World told the Shakers that they planned to stop communication with them. Silence between the two worlds began after May 6, 1844. Before the Spirits left them, the Shaker Community was made aware that the Spirits would return in 1848 and the spiritual gifts would be "poured out in mighty floods upon the world's people as stupendous tokens of spiritual presence." They were also told of "treasures of mineral wealth from the earth's mines that would complement the downstreaming spiritual riches."

These prophecies came into being. In 1848, the Gold Rush began in California. On March 31, 1848, communication took place between Catherine (Katie) and Margaretta (Maggie) Fox and the Spirit of Charles B. Rosna, the murdered peddler who had been buried in the cellar of their cottage at 1510 Hydesville Road, Hydesville, New York. This was just about 100 miles from Watervliet where the new era was first made known and just a few miles south of Sodus Point where a Shaker Community existed.

The decline of the Shakers came about because of an ideological challenge that threatened the view of celibacy. This was the destruct button for the Shaker communities. After Mother Ann's transition, her followers organized the United Society of Believers in Christ's Second Appearing.

The Shakers had accepted what became known as Modern Spiritualism, including all phases of its phenomena. They were well aware of communication long before the event occurred in Hydesville. Sir Arthur Conan Doyle reported that "although the 66 Shaker communities accepted communication, they kept it solely to themselves."

Spiritualism as a Science

In his book entitled the "Arcana of Nature," Hudson Tuttle attempted to make it understood how closed-minded secular science was in regard to Spiritualism as a science. For example, he expressed the reactions of Sir David Brewster. Who was this man? He was a noted inventor, mathematician, philosopher and prominent scientist. Tuttle states that when Sir David Brewster, in a séance saw a table rise from the carpet, Brewster cautiously said, "It seems to rise." He just could not be honest and simply admit what his own eyes witnessed.

Tuttle was exceptionally keen in his insights. He wrote, "...As a Science, Spiritualism is the knowledge of the psychical or spiritual nature of man; and as Spirit, it is the moving force of the universe; its study is that of Creation and is not complete until the unknown becomes known. The Science of Spiritualism is the knowledge of spiritual laws and forces, in their grandest generalizations, as special forms, as limited by individualization in man. It comprises all the relationships individuals sustain in immortal life, and the broader intercourse of the immortal spheres. ...Spiritualism—the philosophy and science of life, here and hereafter; the sum of all truth and incentive to righteousness; we will nail it there, that no hand desecrate it. There it will remain when all the fads and 'olgoies have passed and been forgotten. They are for time but it is without limit or duration."

Before 1848, there is the historical recording that "there would be an extraordinary discovery of material as well as spiritual wealth. Mines of treasure were to be discovered in the earth and floods of spiritual light were to descend from the heavens that would continue until about 1870, when fresh sensuous and supersensuous demonstrations were to proclaim the inauguration of another era."

Prior to the Hydesville event Andrew Jackson Davis, the Poughkeepsie Seer, received a most important message. As a teenager, he was found to have extraordinary gifts. William Livingston, a local tailor experimenting with mesmerism, recognized Davis' talent and continued to work with him in an attempt to unfold his special sight and his diagnosing weaknesses of the physical body. It was from this humble beginning that Davis went into the work. He established his Harmonial Philosophy organization, became a noted orator and author of numerous books.

Davis was given the title of "the John the Baptist of Modern Spiritualism." One of the reasons he is always mentioned in the movement of Spiritualism is because of the important communication he received on the morning of March 31, 1848. Davis said, "About daylight this morning, a warm breathing passed over my face and I heard a voice, tender and strong, saying 'Brother, the good work has begun—behold a living demonstration is born.' I was left wondering what was meant by such a message."

11

III

Hydesville and
The Fox Family

In the very late 1700s settlers took root in the farmlands of an area that one day became known as Hydesville. Considering relocating and continuing his medical practice in a new locale, Henry Hyde, a medical doctor, left Milton, Vermont seeking to find land in Ohio. His search was unsuccessful, and he returned to Vermont. During his travels, the spaciousness of western New York caught his eye.

Reviewing the notes of his long itinerary, he decided to seek out properties in Western, New York. He located a large parcel of fertile farm land near Lyons, New York. Following a visit to the property on September 6, 1819, he purchased the 3,000 acres from William Winters. It was rich land with rolling hills. Dr. Hyde's definitive plans began by having the land cleared and construction of a one and a half-story wooden cottage upon a stone-wall foundation. It was separated from the road-way by a wood-rail fence. In 1815, Dr. Hyde named the new community after his family name — Hydeville. Later the name was changed to Hydesville. The hamlet is about five miles northwest of the village of Newark, Arcadia, Wayne County and was formed from the town of Lyons on February 15, 1825. The address of the house constructed on the corner of Hydesville and Parker Road was designated as 1510 Hydesville Road.

It appears that Dr. Hyde should have made an in-depth study of the area rather than just search for a substantial parcel of land. Because of the lack of a thorough investigation, Dr. Hyde's plans for his medical practice didn't materialize. The sparse population just would not support a medical practice in that location. Unable to survive as a medical practitioner, he sought other avenues to create income. Although the community began to grow with many frame dwellings, a Methodist church and graveyard, a few shops and several businesses, it still seemed to be lacking. With the construction of the Erie Canal, traffic going westward increased. Dr. Hyde soon recognized there was a need for a stopping place for the weary westward traveler. To fill that need, he opened a tavern across the street from the corner of Hydesville and Parker Road. It was a very successful venture that he managed until his transition in 1828.

Dr. Hyde's son, Artemas W., was born in the cottage on September 15, 1816. Years later, after his father had made his transition, Artemas managed his father's accumulation of property and businesses including the rental cottage at 1510 Hydesville Road. Although several families had lived there, interest in the house remains regarding the last three tenants. From 1843 to 1844, the cottage was occupied by John Bell and his wife. It was about a week after the peddler stopped by the Bells to sell his wares that Lucretia, the housekeeper, fell into a fresh hole in the soft earth of the cellar. Mrs. Bell passed it off as rat holes. However, there were also unexplained noises disturbing them day and night. Lucretia became very unhappy and returned home. Soon after her departure, the Bells moved out of the cottage.

From 1846 to 1847, the cottage was rented by Michael Weekman, his wife Hannah, two young daughters and a housekeeper named Janie. Knocks were heard on the door, but no one was there. They continued to be disturbed by the raps and knocks. Finally, they were forced to move out due to the noises of the unseen guests and the severe frightening of their youngest daughter.

The Fox family was planning to move from the house they were renting in Rochester into a new house of their own to be constructed in Hydesville on the property owned by their son. Because of the severe winter weather, construction had to wait until Spring. However, on December 11, 1847, a blustery cold day, the family consisting of John, his wife Margaret Smith Fox and two youngest daughters Margaretta (Maggie) and Catherine (Katie), took residency in the cottage just two miles from David's farm. It is noted that the disturbances occurred from day one and became increasingly worse as days passed into weeks and months.

The stories of happenings on March 31, 1848 have been told over and over again, often being embellished until it has become a very convoluted story. The first and accurate documentation of the incident was authored by Attorney E. E. Lewis. It is entitled *A Report of the Mysterious Noises, Heard in the House of Mr. John D. Fox, in Hydesville, Arcadia, Wayne County, Authenticated by the Certificates and Confirmed by the Statements of the Citizens of that Place and Vicinity* dated April 20, 1848. This was followed by a book entitled "Explanation and History of the Mysterious Communion with Spirits Comprehending the Rise and Progress of Mysterious Noises in Western New York Generally Received as Spirit Communication" by Eliab W. Capron and Henry D. Baron, 1850.

There are two other books authored by two famous pioneers of Spiritualism that provide accurate documentation. Emma Hardinge authored "Modern American Spiritualism," published in 1869. In particular, Chapters II through IV relate to the Fox Sisters and Hydesville.

Mary (Mercy) E. Cadwallader authored a small, accurate book entitled "Hydesville in History," published in 1917. From that time on the facts have been modified many, many times and in some instances, became just a story.

In brief, the Fox family suffered the same disturbances as did the Weekman family. They voiced the same questions that were asked by the Weekmans, "Why can't we have any peace and why did we ever move here?" The noises increased as days passed to weeks and weeks into months. On March 31, 1848, after the family had retired, the rapping increased. It was just about midnight when little nine-year old Katie snapping her fingers asked "Can you count to three?" Immediately the unseen created three distinct raps. Not to be left out, her 11 1/2-year old sister, Maggie chimed in by clapping her hands a number of times. Once again, the unseen accurately obliged. Mrs. Fox was familiar with Spirit communication. She had often sat in séances held by her mediumistic sister, Elizabeth. Mrs. Fox began to question the unseen. She was able to verify that the rappings were created by a 31-year old Jewish peddler who had been murdered in the cottage. He was a husband and father of five. He claimed it happened about midnight on a Tuesday for the $500.00 he had in his coat pocket. He related that his throat had been slashed and his body was dragged down the steps and interred in the cellar of the cottage.

A neighbor, William Duesler, had lived in the house prior to the Bells. His family had never been disturbed but he took a special interest in the manifestations that were taking place. A committee was formed to investigate the happenings and he was made its chief. He cross-examined not only the previous tenants but also the Spirit of Charles B. Rosna. In his questioning, he received the same information gleaned by Mrs. Fox. The next step was to find the body. Although the men attempted to dig in the cellar, the Ganargua (Mud Creek) that often flooded the lowlands, including this property, foiled their effort.

Three months after the event on March 31st, David held a table-tipping séance at his house. He received the peddler's name as Charles B. Rosner (a few documents indicate David received the name Rosma). Had the age old question "If a man die, shall he live again" been answered? Proof of the continuity of life was clearly demonstrated by the peddler. He broke the shackles of death by communicating with the Fox Family in the cottage at Hydesville by the means of the physical phenomena that became known as Spirit Rappings.

Since David Fox had received the name of the peddler in a table-tipping séance in April 1848, the name Charles B. Rosna has been carried on throughout the years. However, others have had different ideas about it. In 1850, Eliab W. Capron and Henry D. Baron in "Explanation and History of the Mysterious Communion with Spirits: Comprehending the Rise and Progress of the Mysterious Noises in Western New York, Generally Received as Spiritual Communications" recorded the name as Charles "Rasme"—in 1853, Henry Spicer recorded in the *Black Woods-Edinburgh Magazine,* under *Spiritual Manifestations* the name as Charles "Rayn"—in 1860, Robert Owen in his book "Footfalls on the Boundary of Another World" listed the name as "Rosma"—in 1869, Emma Hardinge in "Modern American Spiritualism" listed the name as "Rosna"—and, in April 1879, J. L. Pool published in the *Oswego Daily Times,* the name as "Rosemond". Because of this variety of names, research continues today in search of proof of the accuracy of the peddler's name.

The Cottage and its Benefactors

In "Modern American Spiritualism" written by Emma Hardinge and published in 1869, she states, "The humble frame dwelling at Hydesville looms up into the proportions of a gigantic temple whose foundations are laid in the four corners of the earth... ."

In the popular monthly, *The Progressive Thinker,* William Benjamin "Ben" Hayden proclaimed a special place in history for the peddler. He said,

> "His name should be nailed to the mast-head of every paper published in the interest

of the Cause he represents. I would that his name and accomplished mission were engraved in golden letters upon the title page of every booklet and pamphlet issued for the Spiritual press. It should adorn the walls of every Spiritualist Church and it should be framed as a motto and hung in every Spiritualist home throughout the world."

Time reveals many secrets and so it was with the events in Hydesville. Fifty-four years (1904) after the Advent of Modern Spiritualism, the inner east wall of the cellar of the cottage at 1510 Hydesville Road caved in revealing the skeleton of the peddler and his pack. This proved, without a doubt, that the Fox family had indeed made contact with the unseen side of life. It proved the continuity of life!

Preservation of the cottage became a concern of Mr. Benjamin Bartlett, a Spiritualist from Pennsylvania. To preserve it, in 1916 he had the cottage dismantled and transported to the grounds of the Lily Dale Assembly—a Spiritualist Camp in western New York. The site selected was very special. It was here that the tent of Chief Oskenonton, the famous Mohawk Chief known as Running Deer once stood. He had often held séances in his tent on this sacred ground.

Flory Cotrell, a physical phenomena medium living in Lily Dale Assembly, demonstrated Spirit rappings for the many guests who visited the Camp. Unfortunately in September 1955, an early morning blazing fire reduced the cottage to ashes. The peddler's pack was the *only* item saved from the ferocious flames. It is now on display in the Museum at Lily Dale Assembly, Lily Dale, New York.

On the grounds at Lily Dale where the cottage once stood is a Memorial Park identified by a large brass plaque that reads:

MEMORIAL
TO
THE FOX FAMILY
WHO LIVED IN THE COTTAGE AT THE TIME. MARGARET AND KATIE FOX AGED 9 AND 11 YEARS RECEIVED THE FIRST PROOF OF THE CONTINUITY OF LIFE WHICH WAS THE BEGINNING OF MODERN SPIRITUALISM
MARCH 31, 1848
THIS COTTAGE WAS BOUGHT AND MOVED FROM HYDESVILLE, N.Y., ITS ORIGINAL SITE TO LILY DALE, N.Y. IN MAY 1916 BY
BENJAMIN FRANKLIN BARTLETT

John Drummond

John Drummond was a Spiritualist and businessman from Canada who became a U.S. Citizen. He resided in Newark, New York just a few miles from the cottage he often visited. Now only the stone walls of the cellar remained—its covering the sky. The cottage was gone! Having watched the removal of the cottage caused a deep sadness to come over him. As weeks passed, he became more and more despondent.

At one of our visits with John, I asked him what ever got him started on the idea of rebuilding the cottage. He told me, "One day while I was standing gazing into the open cellar and talking to the thin air, suddenly my mind was struck with a flash of light! I needed two things, a floor plan and boards of that time-period. I immediately took action. Once the house was reassembled in Lily Dale, I visited and drew up an exact floor plan of the original cottage. I took the measurements myself. Next I started my search near and far looking for barns with wood of that time-period. I purchased several, removing the wood one piece at a time—all by myself. Then I hauled them and stacked them on the empty corner lot at the property. You know the guy that killed the peddler built an early mausoleum. I guess he laid the body down next to the outside wall, then built this fake inside wall to hide him." John chuckled.

John continued. "After gathering all the material to reconstruct the cottage, the first thing I had to do was secure some of the outside cellar wall, then restack the huge stones that had caved in along the inside wall, too. What a job! I did it all by myself and let me tell you that stone was very heavy." With a grin on his face he said, "I wasn't old back then, you know."

"Once the cellar walls were secure again, I began building the house on the original foundation. I took it upon myself to get it done; then I moved in. People started coming from everywhere to see the cottage. For a long time, I invited them in and showed them around. I gave them each a pamphlet or newspaper clipping about Hydesville. When I ran out, I gave them whatever literature I could gather, like the old *Summit* magazines. You know the National Spiritualist Association sent me one every month."

Smitty said to John, "So you became the caretaker." John said, "I didn't think of that. One of guys in the group sitting around having a picnic and talking suggested my new title as Caretaker. When they left, I got me a nice piece of cardboard and wrote the words, John Drummond, Caretaker of the Hydesville Cottage, and hung it on my front door. Yes, that's me, John the Caretaker!" He chuckled!

Sometime after the 75th Anniversary Celebration at Hydesville, Mary (aka M. E. or Mercy) Cadwallader had the thought that a monument should be placed on the grounds. She generously donated the stone that was placed in the front of the house to the right of the front door. It read

The Birthplace of Modern Spiritualism
Upon this site stood the Hydesville Cottage
The home of the Fox Sisters
Through whose Mediumship Communication
With the Spirit World was Established
March 31, 1848
There is no death and there are no dead!
December 5, 1927

IV

Spiritualism's Public Debut

Background

After the Fox family moved into David's home, the noises began again. Had it not been for Maggie's 34-year old sister Leah, it all might have faded into the dust right there in Hydesville. Leah felt that the girls should be separated. She suggested taking Katie back to Rochester with her and her 18-year-old daughter Elizabeth (Lizzie). Mr. Fox vehemently objected because of Katie's young age. Leah never gave up— persistence was a noted trait of hers. Failing in that effort, she then suggested that he allow Maggie to go to Rochester with them. After much persuasion by Leah, Mr. Fox finally agreed.

Off to Rochester

Leah, Lizzie and Maggie traveled back to Rochester via the Erie Canal. Raps were heard on the boat. Once the sisters settled in Leah's home in Rochester the raps began again. Leah contacted her friend Eliab Capron and Quaker friends Amy and Isaac Post for assistance in determining what should be done. They instructed her to hold regular sittings with friends and family. At first these sessions were known as Spirit Circles. Later, they became known as séances. Many began to unfold their latent abilities. Time passed and Maggie grew very despondent. She missed her dear younger sister, Katie. The only solution was for Mrs. Fox to take little Katie and rush to Leah's home in Rochester. Once they arrived, the sittings continued. The Spirits told them that these manifestations were not to be confined to them but would go all around the world. By November of 1848, it was decided that Katie would go to the home of Mr. and Mrs. E. W. Capron in Auburn where she could continue her schooling. The Spirit Circles continued in both areas, simultaneously spelling out the same Spirit message urging them to permit the raps so the world would know. But the sisters prayed that this cup of bitterness pass from them. They did not wish to be mediums. In November 1848, the Spirits said, "Since you are constantly disobedient to our requests and obviously opposed to our presence we will leave you, and in all probability withdraw for another generation or seek through other sources for the fulfillment of the high and noble purposes with which this spiritual outpouring has been designed."

At once, the Spirits bid them farewell. It was not long thereafter that they realized they had made a terrible mistake and began to plead for the Spirits' return. Capron and his group visited often hoping that the Spirits had returned but were always disappointed to find they had not. Finally, after pleading by the Fox sisters as well as Capron's group, the Spirits returned and once again urged them to make these phenomena public.

Corinthian Hall

The first pubic demonstration of the phenomena was advertised for Tuesday, November 14, 1849, at the newly constructed Corinthian Hall in Rochester, New York. George Willets and Isaac Post were to attend to the business arrangements. Eliab W. Capron would present the address, the subject being "Rapping Phenomena." Amy Post, along with a few other ladies and Rev. Jarvis, with other well-known citizens were to accompany them to the platform. Maggie, with Leah at her side was to carry on the demonstration. During this time, Katie remained in Auburn at the Capron home. As the sisters awaited the time to step onto the stage into the limelight of the world at Corinthian Hall, the first investigation of the science of Spiritualism began. This was not a scientific investigation by laboratory standards, but nonetheless, it was its humble beginning as a science. The first question at that time was *"By what means are the raps produced?"* The second was *"Are these children faking it all?"*

A committee of gentlemen was appointed to investigate the phenomena. Upon completion of the lecture, the phenomena were to be demonstrated. Selected ladies of the gentlemen were assigned the task of searching the sisters. This involved examining them by disrobing them and causing them great embarrassment. Maggie and Leah were petrified. However the result of the demonstrations revealed the fact that they, by no means were involved in any prepared fakery. Due to failure on the part of the committees who were afraid of the lynching crowd, the sessions were held for the second and third time. Once again a group of appointed ladies investigated the clothing, shoes, stockings and under-garments of the weeping child and her adult sister. After that demonstration, the sisters became known as the *Rochester Rappers*. Many that were connected with the press in various cities joined in the investigation and reported in favor of the honesty and truth of the Mediums. But the bitterness of those opposed contin-ued to rage on. Amy and Isaac Post, who had always come to the sisters' rescue, took them to their home and offered them protection. This first public appearance of the Fox Sisters at Corinthian Hall opened the doorway for Modern Spiritualism to become known as a Science. Spirit communication was indeed a fact.

From the described beginnings, things didn't get any easier for Spiritualists. Eliab W. Capron said, "In the first struggle to introduce Spiritualism in all the cities and towns of the United States, a mere glance at the facts and occurrences would make of itself a library of respectable size. But in the first struggle to introduce it when it was not only a novelty but a thing everywhere spoken against, there were occurrences and trials which should be given to the world to be read by future generations. They were declared insane and treated as such for the same cause. Friends were alienated, neighbors tabooed, customers forsook the Spiritualists and these were but some of the wrongs inflicted on some of the early believers." It was difficult then and remains so today to hear the clergy of many denominations defame and deny Spiritualism's phenomena, yet continue to expound upon the teachings of the Apostle Paul, particularly in reading the scripture identified in 1st Corinthians, Chapter 12, Verse 1: "Now, concerning spiritual gifts, brethren, I would not have you ignorant."

It was because of this public demonstration in Corinthian Hall in Rochester that the movement began to unfold into the Heyday of Spiritualism:

1851

- Judge Edmonds formed the New York Circle.
- Leah Fox Fish Brown became a resident of New York City. Maggie and Katie's demonstrations of mediumship became extremely popular in the City.
- New York Conference established.

1852

- ⚘ In Cleveland Ohio, the Fox sisters provided demonstrations and rapped out a message from Dr. Benjamin Franklin.
- ⚘ Maria B. Hayden, a medium and healer, took Spiritualism to England.
- ⚘ The first Society of Philadelphia was founded.
- ⚘ The *Spiritual Telegraph* first published.
- ⚘ Jonathan Koons and John Tipple constructed the first spirit rooms (séance room).

1853

- ⚘ President Abraham Lincoln tracked down the famed medium John Conklin and established regular sittings with him.
- ⚘ Regular meetings were held in Stuyvesant Institute in Brooklyn, New York and at Dodsworth Hall in New York City.
- ⚘ In a sitting with the Fox Sisters, the Hon. Nathaniel P. Tallmadge received authentic communication from John C. Calhoun in his own handwriting. He also received messages by raps.
- ⚘ Daniel D. Home demonstrated levitation in Boston.

1854

- ⚘ The 33rd Congress of the U.S.A. received a document from the Spiritualists with more than 12,000 signatures entitled "A Memorial" requesting that the science of Spiritualism be investigated.

Ex-Governor Nathaniel P. Tallmadge's signature headed the list.

1859

- Robert Owen, the great philanthropist, converted to Spiritualism because of the mediumship demonstrated by Maria B. Hayden. She was known as a test medium.
- Robert Dale Owen published "Footfalls on the Boundary of Another World."

1863

- Dr. Robert Hare, in an attempt to debunk Spiritualism, actually convinced himself of its truth. He re-designed Isaac Peace's Spiritual Telegraph Dial and named his new model Professor Hare's Dial or the Spirit-o-scope.

1866

- The first Spiritualist Camp founded—Pierpont Grove in Massachusetts.

1868

- Dr. J. R. Newton, a noted healer, was a channel for many remarkable healings.
- 20th Anniversary of Modern Spiritualism

1869

☞ As the result of a spirit message, James Lawrence of Ohio proposed establishing a day to celebrate the Anniversary of Modern Spiritualism. The delegates assembled in Convention voted in the affirmative.

1870

☞ The first celebration of the Anniversary of Modern Spiritualism was held around the world.

☞ The first group of organized Spiritualists was the American Spiritualist Association, Victoria Woodhull President.

1893

☞ Spiritualists in the United States joined together under one umbrella by organizing the National Spiritualist Association.

1898

☞ 100th Anniversary of Modern Spiritualism

The Heyday of Spiritualism's first 50 years became history. Spiritualism marched ever onward in the new 20th Century.

V

The Prevatt Settlement

By the mid-1800s, Volusia County had become the hub of many new settlements. Its beauty and climate was a major attraction. In 1858, James H. Prevatt formed a simple, yet elegant 340-acre settlement four miles southeast of Deland. His family settled in a log cabin which was the only dwelling place available in the area. Its outstanding features were it had a wide porch and a clay chimney. The hills and dales, lakes, tall oaks and fields of pines were inviting. When in season, the orange and fig trees offered a sweet aroma. The decorative crepe myrtle and oleanders bloomed everywhere.

In 1868, Prevatt was made a County Judge. At other times he served as County Treasurer and Superintendent of Schools. In 1876, he built his first General Store and a Post Office and established himself as the Postmaster. The settlement developed as an industrial community as well as an agricultural community. It produced cotton, corn, strawberries, figs and oranges. The Prevatt Settlement quickly became known as the place to go in Florida.

In 1884 after the transition of Prevatt, Henry Deland purchased the beautiful 340-acre lake-front property. By the end of the first year, he expanded it to a 1,000-acre settlement. He named it Lake Helen after his lovely daughter, Helen Parce Deland. His dream always was a town of beauty and industry. For many years, Lake Helen embraced the title of *The Gem City of Volusia County* and later, *the Gem City of Florida.*

Mr. Deland financed construction of an extremely large hotel surrounded with towering pines on Lakeview Drive and named it The Harlan House after his son. Later, it became known as the Harlan Hotel. It opened on Thanksgiving eve in 1884. It had three verandas. The long wings to the north and south were completed in 1886 and 1887 respectively. It was very expansive and became an extremely popular resort—a center of social activities. The hotel had its own boathouse with a fleet of brightly colored boats. Another interesting note about Henry Deland is that he was the founder of Stetson University in Deland, Florida.

In 1886, the area attracted many more visitors after E. R. Chapman completed the Atlantic and Western Railway meandering easterly across the county to New

Smyrna on the east coast of Florida. The name was later changed to the Florida East Coast Railway System. Lake Helen became a major railroad station. Its trains not only transported the winter guests but handled the shipping for many of the industrial businesses in Lake Helen.

Another attraction of the area was warm weather for the winter guests from the north. Tourism became extremely popular, particularly because of warm winter months.

Dr. O. B. Webster was well respected in the medical field. His Sanitarium on Macy Street in Lake Helen was often recommended by professional medical doctors through-out the country to those suffering various pulmonary ailments. The resin of the tall pines also provided heal-ing energies and, in some cases was necessary for a cure. It is noted that an article in the *Banner of Light* stated that George P. Colby's doctor recommended he go to Florida to receive relief in his suffering from tubercu-losis, a pulmonary disease.

The area was also gaining in industrial growth at an extremely fast pace. For instance, there was J. G. Sheldon's General Store, Dr. J. C. Mill's Drug Store, Bond's Veneer Factory, Bond's Sandstone & Brick Company and later a Bond Store selling clothing, shoes, furniture and rugs. The Starch Factory in the early 1900s made starch from coontie fern. The firm of Broadman and

Davis started a Saw Mill along with three other mills and Albert Baher set up a nursery with 60,000 orange trees. There was a packing house, barber shop, school house, U. S. Post Office, several banks, an outdoor movie and various medical practices. Religion played a big part in Lake Helen with the construction of several churches—the Blake Memorial Baptist Church (1864) that later changed to Euclid Avenue Baptist Church, the First Congregational Church (1886) and the Methodist Episcopal Church (1923). The rapid growth of the town was phenomenal.

The two-story Harlan House with its stately verandas had a full booking year-after-year. Due to the increase in winter guests, more housing was needed. This issue was resolved by the construction of the handsome two-story Euclid Hotel on the corner of Euclid and Main Street in Lake Helen. M. L. Granville was the proprietor. The name was later changed to the Granville Hotel. An article in the local weekly newspaper, *Life in Florida,* stated that it had 2,000 winter guests its first year in operation. The location of the railroad station offered easy travel. Once again, more tourist arrivals called for additional rooms in the area. In 1898 the Huffs, a niece and nephew of Maude Smith, had another hotel constructed facing the Lake that was later named Lake Colby. The hotel was known as the Webster Hotel.

Change brought along an undesired aspect. The railroad's expansion in a southerly direction was a detriment to the Lake Helen community. Tourism decreased. The tourists now sought the latest attractions—Fort Lauderdale and Miami. As time passed, the Harlan House became rundown, and although a new owner remodeled it, a blazing fire destroyed it on Halloween night, October 31, 1922. At other times, fires put the Granville Hotel and the Webster Hotel into oblivion.

PART II

VI

Ever Onward

The Colby Story

Spiritualism continued to grow in the United States and abroad. It was also doing very well in Great Britain and its territories. There were Home Circles, Churches, Camps and independent organizations. At this point in time we introduce George Prescott Colby and the part he played in the promulgation of Modern Spiritualism.

George Prescott Colby was born the son of James and Elmina A. Lewis Colby in the small town of Pike, Wyoming County, New York, on January 6, 1848. His siblings were two brothers James L. and Martin E. and two sisters, Eugenia and Julia. According to the official records, his first and primary occupation was that of a school teacher. In 1870, he worked as a tailor. However for a major part of his life, he was involved in spiritual activities throughout the United States and Canada. From 1881-1884 he traveled from east to the west Coast of the United States serving in the Washington territory, East Oregon and San Francisco. In 1886 he served in Victoria, British Columbia. He resided in California for a short time.

It was during his early years, that he was introduced as a bright, young lad. At the time of his baptism at age 12, he received a message from his uncle who had received a spirit message through a medium that George was a medium and predicted he would found a camp in the Southern States. At that young age, George demonstrated mediumship with the assistance of a Native American Indian Spirit Guide named Seneca. His consciousness was expanded by a German Guide known as The Philosopher. He was blessed with Wandah, a guide with healing, and he also became aware of the wisdom of Professor Hoffman. George P. Colby was known for his ability to provide excellent demonstrations of clairvoyance as well as being an instrument for spiritual healing. In his later years he became an eloquent orator. His favorite word was Tranquilidad. It came from the Spanish term meaning a clear conscience and, in the English meaning tranquility, calmness and peace.

At this point we strive to separate fact from fiction. Various stories were introduced and embellished down through the years. It is well documented that in 1875, Colby as a young man was engaged as a trance medium at a séance in the home of S. D. Wadsworth in Lake

Mills, Iowa. A message from the Spirit side of life told him that he should go to Eau Clair, Wisconsin and meet with Theodore D. Giddings and, at that time, further instructions on an important matter would be given. A short time later, Colby followed the instructions. He met with Giddings in Eau Claire and it is told that during a séance it was revealed that a Spiritualist Camp was to be established in the south and that Colby was to be instrumental in its founding. Shortly thereafter, preparations were made for the trip. Giddings, Colby and 25 others traveled by rail to Chicago, south to Tallahassee and arrived in Jacksonville, Florida. From there they enjoyed a long, long ride on The Volusia, a wood-burning steamboat, down the St. Johns River to Blue Springs. On November 1st, they docked at Stark Landing on the lower side of Blue Springs near Orange City. They stayed in an old palmetto shed along with other travelers. Colby's guide Seneca was to have told them the camp would be in the vicinity of Blue Springs. From here, the story varies. One account records that

> They followed a foot path for a little distance, then straight through the deep forest. They went for several miles until at last standing on the ground resembling that of Cassadaga, New York—viewed as the Promised Land. Its high bluffs, lakes and the general lay of the land was a replica of the New York site. Everything was found

exactly as it had been described by Colby's guide before leaving Wisconsin.

The next story is

...Colby first stepped foot on land at Enterprise, Florida. While traveling through the woods with an Indian he had met at Blue Springs, he located property that reminded him of Cassadaga, New York... .

The third story is

...that George, being sickly with tuberculosis (a pulmonary condition) was recommended by his doctor to go to Florida in an attempt to recover his health.

The latter statement about Colby's health appears to be accurate. The *Banner of Light,* a Spiritualist newspaper of the day, did carry an article stating that Colby's doctor had recommended he go to Florida—the land of pines was particularly encouraging for those suffering from tuberculosis.

In any event, no matter how George P. Colby arrived in Lake Helen is of minor importance. The fact simply is that at some point in time he arrived by mule at Jenks Place, just south of where Lake Helen is situated today.

Life Goes On

Colby was given a general picture of the acreage that would be ideal for a camp. However, others were also interested in it and he was encouraged to act fast. Shortly thereafter he learned two men were planning to leave the next day to go to the United States General Land Office in Gainesville. He immediately rented a mule from W. R. Long and headed for Gainesville traveling throughout the night to be assured of foiling their attempt in getting the land.

Colby was successful. The transactions are recorded in the General Land Book Vol. 3 Page 350 and 351; Patent Book O, Page 361-363. Shortly thereafter, Colby christened his acreage Southern Cassadaga. The new community was named after the northern community in New York that he knew so well—Cassadaga, New York. The name Cassadaga is a dialect of the Seneca Indian and is expressed as "Gustavo Tecarneodi" which means rocks beneath the waters. The Seneca Native American Indian Reservation is just seven miles from Cassadaga, New York.

REMAINING STEPS TO COLBY'S HOUSE TODAY

For eight months, George lived in a deserted old log storage crib with his bed of moss covered logs, and an open fire pit, covered by the sky. During that time, his large house was constructed on the west side of the lake. He later named it Lake Colby. As time went on he acquired additional acreage. On April 11, 1911 his house was destroyed in a blaze of fire. A kerosene stove ignited some nearby wood and the flames quickly spread throughout the house. George's persistence prevailed and he had a new house constructed on the same grounds.

Life in those early years in Florida was quite different. Colby traveled by foot to Beresford, 12 miles away or to Enterprise on the St. Johns River for provisions. He traveled to Blue Springs for mail. Of course, livelihood was another issue. Colby was well-known to be humorous, witty, clever, frank, honest and a man of integrity. He did follow Spirit's advice and started very profitable businesses that included a chicken and dairy farm, a small orange grove and lumber business. His teacher instinct made him very fond of children. The story varies as to his fostering from two to 14 orphaned children.

Although Colby named the new community, he did not found the Southern Cassadaga Spiritualist Camp Meeting Association. A few articles in the Spiritualist magazines of the day record that in the early days of his settling the land, clearing the trees and brush and having a house built, he did periodically hold various Spiritualist meetings on his acreage. In the same time sequence, Colby was very proud of his successful business endeavors that included platting part of the acreage and selling various sized parcels. In business, Colby was extremely strict—pay up or give up. On March 15, 1892, Colby sold one large plat of land to Anna Stevens, a long-time resident of Lake Helen. Anna platted out Stevens' subdivision. Stevens Street is a main thoroughfare through downtown Cassadaga and the main street within the campgrounds. Things did not go as Anna had planned. She could not or chose not to fulfill the balance of her mortgage to Colby. It is this land that the group of the members of the Rowley Camp voted upon for their new endeavor. They assumed Steven's mortgage and the Southern Cassadaga Spiritualist Camp Meeting Association became a reality in 1894.

The records in the Court House verify that Colby did donate 50-feet for an access to the property purchased by the group of 13 who had left the De Leon Spring Camp to form the Southern Cassadaga Spiritualist Camp Meeting Association. They had not yet cleared nor established an entrance to their property. Colby offered them his homestead as a place to hold their first Grand Opening Season and they accepted. For a time he served the Camp as a medium and orator.

VII

Spiritualism Comes
to Florida

George P. Colby, the well-known trance orator of
Spiritualism arrived in Florida in 1875. His interest
was primarily for better health conditions and secondly,
providing a livelihood. As the years passed he became
extremely busy in his business ventures and not aware
of what was taking place just 35 miles northwest of
Cassadaga in De Leon Springs, Florida.

A well-known Spiritualist by the name of Dr. William
Rowley was actively establishing the first Spiritualist
camp in Florida. He took all the required precautions to
properly incorporate a non-profit religious organization
naming it The National Spiritual and Liberal Association.

He was well aware that to have an efficient and successful camp that could serve the people, it was necessary
to have the best orators of the philosophy and the best

demonstrators of the phenomena. Dr. Rowley could do his part in serving as a medium for he was well-known as a spirit telegrapher. He needed others to cover the complete spectrum of Spiritualism. As he thought on the matter, George P. Colby came to mind. He knew George was well respected, particularly in the northern Spiritualist sector. He was aware that he could serve well as a trance orator and superb at demonstrating mediumship. He also knew George had many influential northern contacts. They were people highly respected in their chosen field and many were financially endowed. If George was a part of his camp he could bring both talent and wealth to the organization.

Dr. Rowley, being an intelligent man, immediately made his next move in his plan to have a successful and official grand opening of the first camp season January 1, 1894. He met with Colby and offered him the position of President of the Camp. George graciously accepted without hesitation. He immediately took on the task at hand and invited the very best workers from Cassadaga Lake Free Assembly as well as from Michigan, Wisconsin and New England. The calendar schedule listed the most talented orators and mediums, not to mention people who could provide the finances required for growth of a camp—familiar names such as Abby L. Pettengill, Marion and Thomas Skidmore, Harrison D. Barrett, Morris Pratt, Hubbard and Sarah Brigham and others.

Today there are still a few who continue to question a camp in Florida before the Southern Cassadaga Spiritualist Camp Meeting Association's existence. The first proof offered is found documented in the 1893 bound minutes of the founding convention of the National Spiritualist Association of the United States of America, an umbrella for all Spiritualists. Very early in the first session, George P. Colby asked the Chair to read this message. "All parties wishing information concerning the Winter Camp in Florida at De Leon Springs can obtain the same by applying to W. S. Rowley, George P. Colby and E. C. & Julia Hyde."

The De Leon Camp Association continued to expand in numbers and quickly outgrew its property. Much discussion revealed there were differences in opinion as to what areas should be considered for property that would suit their need. It was suggested they look at property in Daytona, Jacksonville, Palatka, St. Petersburg, Tampa and Winter Park. The brothers, John B. and H. H. Clough, generously offered to donate 25 acres of their land that adjoined the camp. They followed this proposal by offering to construct a brick hotel of 200 rooms. Colby and the Clough's never saw eye-to-eye. George sat by in silence as his fury grew within. During discussions it was noted that Colby did a lot of whispering to his friend and neighbor Emma Huff. Of course it was noticed and some wondered what it was all about.

Never doubt the power of women! Emma Huff agreed to follow Colby's suggestion and meet with her friend of many years, the strong-willed Marion Skidmore. Emma told Marion that her guide, Complanter, told her there would be a spiritual center in Florida but it was not to be in De Leon Springs. She went on to suggest that she show Marion the beautiful hills, dales, lakes and tall pines on Colby's land in Lake Helen. Marion agreed to go with Emma, and upon arrival at the area could not believe her eyes. It resembled their beloved Cassadaga, New York and Marion immediately suggested it be named, Southern Cassadaga. She was sure this was a Spirit-led adventure. She was convinced this should be the location of the new camp! The women returned to the De Leon Springs camp and with little trouble, convinced the membership to purchase the property in Lake Helen by assuming Anna Steven's mortgage with Colby.

Timeline of events:
General Land Book, Vol 3, Page 350-351
"United States to George P. Colby, Lot 2, Sec 5. Township 18 SR 31E of Tallahassee Meridian 74 Acres and 44/100. Certificate 1."
Recorded March 28, 1884
and
The County Courthouse, Patent Book 0, Page 361-363
United States to George P. Colby "identifying the tract Lot 1 and 2 N. line No. 5 in Township No. 18."
Recorded March 28, 1884

Mortgage Book 8 Page 566

"George Colby to Anna Stevens, Lots 1 and 2 in Volusia County, Florida Twp 18 S.R. 31 East and containing 149 34/100 acres, more or less; note $2,300.00 due in eight years at 10% interest."
Recorded March 15, 1892

Right-of-Way Deed Book 24, Page 45

Colby to Board of the Southern Cassadaga Spiritualist Camp Meeting Association: "50 foot right-of-way North line of Sec. 5 Twp 18 SR 31 East and Extension south-wardly 1306 feet more or less recorded...25 feet on each side of East Line of Lot 2 of Sec. 5 Township 18 SR 31-use as a street as long as the Camp was an Assembly."
Recorded January 28, 1895

Warranty Deed Book 23, Page 224

Colby to Southern Cassadaga Spiritualist Camp Meeting Association Warranty Deed: "East line of Lot 2 Sec. 5 Township 18 SR 31 East begin at point 1306 feet South of N. E. Corner of said Lot 2 being 35 acres of Lot 2 more or less."
Recorded January 28, 1895

Assumption of Mortgage Book 8 Page 566

Southern Cassadaga Spiritualist Camp Meeting Association to Colby: "Association agreed to pay as a void and subsistence indebtedness of said Association

unpaid portion of note and mortgage given by Colby to
Stevens Mortgage Book 8, Page 566."
Recorded April 13, 1895

To date, the only property found to have been donated
to the Southern Cassadaga Spiritualist Camp Meeting
Association by George P. Colby was the 50 foot
right-of-way.

VIII

Cassadaga, Florida

On The Map

The Southern Cassadaga Spiritualist Camp Meeting Association was born December 18, 1894 as a non-profit stockholder corporation at Christmas, Titusville, Florida. It became known as the sister camp to the Cassadaga Lake Free Assembly (CLFA) in Cassadaga, New York, today known as the Lily Dale Assembly. Colby did not sign the incorporation document for the new camp stating that Seneca told him not to sign it but remain in the background. The 13 original founders of the SCSCMA were Spiritualists who left The National Spiritual and Liberal Association that was established by Dr. William Rowley in De Leon Springs. They were Thomas and Marion Skidmore, Abby L. Pettengill, Emma J. Huff, Frank Bond, Harvey W. Richardson, Aldailla C. Jewett, Jerry Robinson, Mariette Cuscaden, Soledad B. Sofford, George W. Liston, George and Maria H. Webster. The 1895 Mortgage Book 8 Page 566 states "they assumed

the indebtedness of Anna Stevens to George P. Colby"
and the Warranty Deed for 35 acres is in Deed Book 23,
Page 224 Recorded January 28, 1895.

The purpose of the camp was to

- provide for and maintain and hold assemblages,

- hold meetings for literary, scientific, philosophical,
  moral and religious instruction,

- encourage establishments of schools, libraries and
  sanitariums,

- ordain and license ministers,

- encourage branch camps in Florida and the
  Atlantic Gulf Coast,

- engage speakers, instructors and other such per-
  sons to further the cause of Modern Spiritualism
  and to especially teach the doctrine of immortality
  of the soul, the nearness of the Spirit World, the
  guardianship of Spirit loved ones and friends and
  the possibility of Spirit communication.

With all the formal legalities in order, it was time
to get down to work. One item was the completion of
a draft layout of the camp. The next official business

was recognizing the need to amend the original charter of the SCSCMA. After meetings and discussions, an amendment was approved by the Judge in the Chambers at Deland on July 16, 1895. It provided for revisions of Articles VI, X, and XI as follows:

- ☞ Article VI detailing the management of the association by a Board of seven and their related power for specific actions.

- ☞ Article X established the dollar value of real estate allowed to be held and

- ☞ Article XI established the total stock and shares of the association. It was recorded on July 16, 1895.

The acreage for the camp was woodlands of tall pines amongst the lakes and ponds. Access to the property was needed. In Volusia County Courthouse Book 24, Page 45 records Colby gave the Camp property for a 50-foot right-of-way to "use as long as the Camp was an Assembly." It was named Marion Street, perhaps after Marion Skidmore. When Stevens had platted out the land, the main street east and west was Denton Avenue and north and south Stevens Street.

The first meeting of the SCSCMA was held on January 15, 1895 at George Webster's place. The second meeting for the official opening of the camp was scheduled at the George P. Colby homestead. He borrowed a tent from the East Coast Railways for the three-day meeting. The First Season officially opened with a Flag Raising Ceremony on February 8, 1895. Just a little more than 100 people attended.

The area designating the SCSCMA boundaries was completely fenced in with a main gatehouse and gate on the corner of what is now Marion Street and Cassadaga Road, SR 4139. Visitors to the camp paid an entrance fee of 10¢ a day or $2.50 for the season. The residents were identified by special entry passes.

The early settlers agreed the land that was to become the Camp was chosen from both the spiritual and mortal sides of life. It was not to be a camp like many of the northern camps—a city unto itself. Rather, it was to be a winter home for the northern Spiritualists who desired to escape the cold winters and be able to continue their practice of Spiritualism. It was not only to be known as a camp but as an educational center where the student of philosophy and religion could better understand the purposes of life here as well as the life hereafter.

Capital Stock, Book of Incorporations 1, Page 12 states "The capital stock of the Association shall be $25,000 divided into shares of $10.00 each... ."
Recorded July 16, 1895.

The very first winter the northern Spiritualists, many from the Cassadaga Lake Free Assembly, housed themselves in tents on Marion Street. Shortly thereafter, some of them began to build cottages along Marion Street and soon expanded to Stevens Street. Although it was advertised the weather was much like the northern month of June, it did get chilly and it was suggested some warm garments should be brought with them. It was recommended that a stove be installed in each house because 'the days do often turn cool.' The small cottages were soon embraced with some large elegant houses constructed on the land leased to them by the Association. A 99-year lease had the meaning of "as if to own." Only a few of the large homes and one hotel remain standing today. In 1896, Abby Pettengill and Emma Huff operated a hotel on the grounds.

The map of 1902 displays some of the cottages that replaced the tents that once lined Marion and Stevens Streets. Other camp members built big homes outside of the camp boundaries because they did not want to place their expensive homes on leased land nor be forced to abide by restrictions, such as "no dogs allowed" or "no alcoholic beverages permitted."

The construction on the grounds took its direction from the northern camps—a library, post office, pavilion and a gazebo as a meeting place. A popular contractor in the area by the name of Purdy took on the nickname of "T.

C." Purdy. The name was derived from the fact that most of the structures he was responsible for constructing had tin roofs and cement walls, thus the initials T. C.

Eber W. Bond moved to Deland in 1881. He founded the E. W. Bond Company with his three sons as partners. He was known as a crusader for good roads. Frank E. and Robert M. Bond founded the Bond Sandstone & Brick Company of Lake Helen. In 1904, they obtained rights to control a valuable German patent that gave them exclusive rights of manufacturing the brick within the state of Florida. Bond's Company not only was responsible for the sturdy bricked roads in the Camp but also shipped brick to other areas in the United States. The train station in Lake Helen made this possible. Many local buildings were constructed with their brick, such as Carnegie Library at Stetson University in Deland. As recent as 1989, a brick walk-way was uncovered on the west and south side of the Burley residence on Bond Street. County employees digging on the corner of Lake and Stevens Street exposed more of the brick. Today, there is still some of the brick exposed in various areas of the camp grounds.

There was construction and more construction. The camp was growing in various shapes and forms of architecture. Marion Skidmore, who was known to promote education, suggested the idea for a very fine library. It was situated to the right of the hotel. The library was one of the main attractions of the camp. A Pavilion and a Grocery Store faced the lake just to the south of the three-story Cassadaga Hotel. All of them along with the Cassadaga Hotel succumbed to the blazing fire on Christmas Eve 1926.

The beauty of the area brought many to Cassadaga. The lovely majestic Rose Garden was maintained by the ladies of the Camp. They had the largest and most productive rose garden in this part of the state. Many people drove miles to Cassadaga just to enjoy the beauty of the magnificent rose garden.

The early settlers were some of the most revered pioneers of Modern Spiritualism including the Brighams, Twings, Thatchers, Websters, and Bonds—J. Clegg Wright, the famous medium—Buchanan the psychometrist—Boddington, the author and Morris Pratt, the educationist who built the first school for Modern Spiritualism in Wisconsin. Today, the school is the only such facility in the United States.

As time went on 15 acres of a tall pine grove facing the lake became a part of the SCSCMA, making a total of 50 acres. By 1902, it was recorded with additional purchase the total was increased to 55 acres. A bathhouse was erected at the lake for the convenience of the swimmers.

In 1895, the Brighams from Fitchburg, Massachusetts erected a very large cottage on Marion Street.

Harmony Hall

It was soon recognized that there must be a place for guests to remain on the grounds. In 1896, a two-story apartment building was constructed facing Stevens Street and named Harmony Hall. It provided for light housekeeping. It was constructed of suites of three rooms to be rented separately or together. A kitchen in the center accommodated those renting rooms on either side. The rooms were 12 x 14 feet in size and furnished with beds, pillows, comfortable chairs and one rocker, table and lamp. The kitchen had one cook stove with two sets of furniture, two brooms and two dust-pans. By 1901, the rates for these rooms with one-half of the kitchen were from $2 to $3 per week, according to location. The suites of three rooms were rented for the entire winter for $35-$40 paid in advance and one room with one-half kitchen for half price. By 1910, the rental of a three-room suite was $3.00 a week or $55 a season paid in advance. By 1926, the fee was $150 a season!

Brigham Hall

In 1897, Dr. Hubbard H. and Sarah C. Brigham, both eclectic medical doctors along with Fred and Kate Brigham, had an apartment building constructed just behind their cottage on Marion Street, and across from Harmony Hall on Stevens Street. They named it Brigham

Hall. The building had 18 single rental rooms—20 rooms in all. For many years, the building was fully occupied. The overflow of guests slept on quilts on the attic floor.

BRIGHAM HALL

Fred and Kate sold their interest to Sarah Brigham. At the passing of her heirs in 1912, it was sold to Frank and Mary Phelps. In 1913 the Association purchased it for $1,500. In 1928, Brigham Hall was remodeled creating the 18 rooms into four private 3-room apartments with private bath and remains so today. The attic is used for tenant storage. As time went on more housing became a necessity and residents rented out their spare rooms. Tents were permitted in the back area of the Campground. As the Camp continued to grow, all of the establishments were full to capacity.

An article in the *Banner of Light,* January 6, 1900 states the Camp residents were obsessed with signs such as '"No Trespassing"—"Fire Exit"—"No Parking"—"Open"—"Closed"—"Medium In"—"Medium Out"—"Not Available"—"Air Conditioned"—"Heated" and "Proper Dress Required."

Railroads & Steamship

The shortest rail travel from the mid-western states and Cincinnati to Lake Helen was provided by two routes. They were: the Queen and Crescent Route and the other the Louisville & Nashville (L&N). During camp season, special service was run by the Northwest line and its connections. One could leave Cincinnati in the morning and arrive at Lake Helen the afternoon of the next day.

Transportation was available at low excursion rates for the wind-solid vestibule trains with sleeping cars with no change of cars from Cincinnati to Jacksonville. On daylight trains, observation, café and parlor cars were available from Cincinnati and Chattanooga.

Mallory Steamship Line provided a cheaper excursion route traveling from New York City to Florida. It ran from October through January.

Water System

From the inception of the Camp, the Association always supplied good clear, tasty water for the residents and guests. Three deep-rock wells were drilled and water piped to a large tank on Prospect Hill just west of Chauncey Street. A gasoline engine and windmill supplied the power to distribute the water through the pipe lines to all of the cottages and public buildings. Bits and pieces of the tower remain in the wooded area just northwest of the Slater house.

Years later, Slater was responsible for donating and developing a water plant near the wooded area just off Marion Street and behind the Temple. The water was routinely analyzed to assure there were no impure elements. Cassadaga water was so good it became a luxury. Clients of the mediums and other guests to the Camp came with as many empty jugs as they could carry to take home some of the best water in Florida. The plant continued serving the community until the 1990s when the Board of Directors of the Association sold the water plant to the County for $40,000. Today, Volusia County furnishes the water to the residents and businesses at a monthly fee.

The Pavilion

The original Pavilion was situated on Marion Street where part of the Hotel now stands. It housed all of the recreational activities such as ballroom dancing, square dancing, teas, card parties, musicals, theatrics, the Annual Masquerade Ball and general meetings. The pavilion constructed was 75' x 60' with a dance hall of 60' x 60' and three rooms for the Ladies Aid to prepare for dances, card parties, supplies and all social affairs. That hall succumbed to the fiery blaze of 1926.

Once it was reconstructed on Stevens Street, it was known as the Pavilion or Recreation Hall. Dances were held regularly drawing people from the neighboring towns. During World War II the sailors stationed in nearby towns frequented the dances. The Ladies Aid Society made all the provisions for the social affairs held in the hall. In 1974, the first major renovation of the hall took place to the style building seen today. The ceiling was lowered, walls paneled, updated electrical wiring and a new roof put in place. A small room became the library.

In 1976, the Board of the Association thought some honor should be given Emanuel Swedenborg or Andrew Jackson Davis who they understood to be The Father of Modern Spiritualism. Davis won out and they renamed the Hall the Andrew Jackson Davis building. Many were not and are not aware of the fact that in his sequel to his autobiography, "Beyond the Valley," he clearly divorces himself from the Cause, stating he was not a Spiritualist and stated, "I align with the Spiritualism's philosophy only to the degree it aligns with my Harmonial

Philosophy"—the organization that he had founded. Davis is credited for the message he is said to have received on the morning of March 31, 1848, "About daylight this morning a warm breathing passed over my face and I heard a voice, tender and strong, saying, 'Brother, the good work has begun—behold, a living demonstration is born.' I was left wondering what could be meant by such a message."

The question is often asked, How did A. J. Davis get the title Father of Modern Spiritualism? He gained the title in the midst of a heated debate with an Episcopalian minister. When it appeared that the Episcopal minister was losing the debate, frantically and in a negative and derogatory tone called Davis the "Father of Modern Spiritualism."

Davis was personal friends with many of the first group of Spiritualists that organized in Philadelphia, Pennsylvania. He did give freely of his services to their philosophical discussions. After his first wife and daughter had made their respective transitions, he married Mary Love, a dedicated Spiritualist. Davis supported her affiliation and, in that respect, he often attended the philosophical discussions and presented philosophical dissertations, such as his *Declaration of Spiritual Independence.*

In the summer and fall of 1985, the Andrew Jackson Davis Building was renovated again. The kitchen was brought up to date, the ladies room enlarged and a closet/pantry area created into a men's room

ANDREW JACKSON DAVIS BUILDING

The Camp Bookstore and Gift Shop

As the Camp continued to grow, there became a need for a larger book store. Spiritualist Camps and Churches have always had book tables in their facilities. From the 1950s onward, selected books and pamphlets restricted to the Science, Philosophy and Religion of Spiritualism were sold from a large ornate table in the rear of the Auditorium, now the Colby Memorial Temple. As more books were coming onto the market, it was decided to increase the space for the store. With a bit of renovation in 1985, a small book store became operable in the A. J. Davis Building. It was located at the far side of the building in the corner next to what is now the Eloise Page Meditation Garden. The birth of a gift shop came with a few souvenir items.

In the 1990s the building was remodeled and the large hall divided into a meeting hall with the remaining part for the Cassadaga Book Store and Gift Shop. More expansion became necessary and today, the larger book-store and gift shop has an experienced manager, Selene Green, who created a successful business for the Camp. It has a select variety of gifts, greeting cards, candles, salt lamps, stones, crystals, jewelry, Native American Indian articles, incense, scrolls, books, magazines and CDs. It also serves as a Welcoming and Informational Center with a joyful staff ready to assist the many vis-itors. Often these guests return to attend the various services, classes and, often, to see a medium. No matter why they come, they never leave without visiting the Cassadaga Book Store and Gift Shop.

The Auditorium

The first open-air Auditorium was constructed in 1897 as an octagonal shaped building situated where the roadway now skirts Seneca Park and just behind the Colby Temple. It was designed by C. E. Parcell of Tampa, Florida. It had wooden benches and a pine needle floor.

Because of its small size, many meetings were held in other areas of the campgrounds.

By 1901 an auditorium was constructed on a bluff over-looking Lake Colby. It had a shingled roof, cloth sides and comfortable seating to house nearly a thousand people. It had a deep and wide platform. At that time it was announced that Sunday services would be held during the Camp season. In 1911 services commenced year round. In 1918, the building was enclosed with large memorial windows donated by the members. Heat stoves were a welcomed addition. Once it was regularly filled to capacity, John Slater, the Camp President, was respon-sible for overseeing the construction of a new brick and cement auditorium located on the corner of Stevens and Marion Street. Some say the Board of Directors chose John Mace architect of Lake Helen to design an audito-rium for their Spiritualist services. Others say Tampa's architect B. Clayton Bonfoey designed the new auditorium bringing a new style of architecture to the community. In 1923, the Bond Sandstone & Brick Company fur-nished the cement and brick, and construction began on the new temple at 1250 Stevens Street. It was named The Auditorium. It was designed to seat 750 people. The floors were constructed sloping downward toward the platform. Connective seating was placed throughout the center and up and down both sides of the structure. The cost of constructing the auditorium was just more than $8,000.00 which was why there was a lengthy delay in completion of it. For many years, the west wall behind the platform was adorned with an attractive large framed picture of Jesus donated by one of the members. It was bordered with rich draperies. Spiritualists then and now revere Jesus as a wayshower—greatest teacher and medium who they frequently quote saying, "Greater things than these ye can do, if you believe." In recent years, the picture was removed and, from time to time, replaced with various paintings and beautiful draperies. The platform presents an appealing and refreshing spiritual atmosphere.

In 1974, the Board of Directors chose to honor George Prescott Colby by changing the name of the temple from The Auditorium to the Colby Spiritualist Temple. In March 1975, the name was changed again to the Colby Memorial Temple as it was thought more suitable. Regardless of name, the building has had some of the greatest orators and mediums of Spiritualism grace its platform, such as the Revs. William Elliott Hammond, Arthur Myers, Harrison D. Engle, Robert Macdonald, D. Mona Berry, Arthur Ford, Maude Kline, Edyth Meader, Helene Gerling and the famous mediums, Jack Kelly, P.L.O.A. Keeler—famous slate-writing medium and the phenomenal mental mediums Mable Riffle, Betty Purcel-Putnam, Mae Graves-Ward and Robert Bos.

In the early days "The Season" schedule was January through March. Later it changed from December through March. Some eager winter guests began arriving as early as November and left as late as April. Today, the SCSCMA functions on a year-round basis.

COLBY MEMORIAL TEMPLE TODAY

The Séance Room

A special note must be made for the Séance Room situated behind the platform of the Auditorium (Colby Memorial Temple). The long rectangular room had a curtain across one end that could be drawn to form a cabinet. The purpose of the cabinet is for the building up of energy and ectoplasm necessary for the medium sitting therein to produce the physical phenomena known as materializations. In the earlier days, some of the most talented mediums participated in authentic demonstrations of physical mediumship, including trumpet, independent voice, materializations and table-tipping. The outstanding slate writer, P.L.O.A. Keeler always held slate-writing séances when on the Campgrounds. *The Sunflower* announced that the 1901 season would have mediums available for materialization, trumpet, trance, writing, healing and tests.

For too many years the room has sat idle except for the strong vibrations of Spirit. Today's parapsychology term for that is "the lingering effect." The popular séances of days gone by seemed as if they would never return as mediumship today fails to meet the demonstrations of yesteryear. This has happened predominantly because the preparation for a good physical phenomena séance requires taking time to sit in the silence to energize body, mind and spirit. Today, our world is much different than in the 19th Century. We live in a busy world connected by all sorts of electronic gear, leaving little time for the peace and silence that energizes. Most classes for unfoldment meet weekly. That hardly provides for a consistency of vibrations required for physical phenomena. There remain a few—very few—authentic demonstrations of physical phenomena in our world of today.

SÉANCE ROOM

In this Age of Aquarius, many are now seeking to bring forth the innate abilities that lie dormant in all of us. Home circles are once again becoming popular because many are now willing to dedicate time and effort to unfoldment. A circle is a place where a medium can unfold their natural talent among like-minded people. As a result, we are beginning to witness flares of ectoplasm, transfiguration and direct voice. Physical phenomena will become a part of this 21st Century.

The Church

The first regularly held church services in Cassadaga were conducted in the Auditorium under the auspices of the National Spiritualist Association in the mid-1940s. The Reverends E. B. and Eloise Page served as NSA ministers for several years. After they left the NSA, the First Spiritualist Church of Cassadaga was chartered by the NSA in the mid-1950s. It rented the Auditorium from the Camp and held its church service every Sunday afternoon from 2:30 to 4:00 P.M. It remained active for more than 25 years. Some of the Pastors that served were the Revs. J. Pacquin, Leland H. Delong, Arthur Myers, Edward Segebrecht, Mae Graves-Ward and James Buchanan. Today the SCSCMA is registered as a Church Corporation and holds its weekly services in the Colby Memorial Temple. There is the regular Sunday Service that includes healing, an oratory and demonstration of mediumship. After the service, lunch is served in the Andrew Jackson Davis Building followed by a one-hour all message service provided by both student and certified mediums. A Wednesday night all-Message Service also provides an avenue for student Mediums to work towards professional certification. Everyone is welcome to all of the services.

Professionals and Music

Spiritualism has a rich history. It began with the *free thinkers* who had a serious Cause—Spiritualism. The Spiritualists participated prominently in every reform of the era. They looked kindly to such as Ingersoll, Emerson and Susan B. Anthony—her name synonymous with woman suffrage. They held in reverence Cora L. V. Richmond, Mary (M. E. Mercy) Cadwallader, Emma Hardinge Britten and Elizabeth Harlow-Goetz.

Many professionals drifted into the Spiritualist movement, bringing their many and varied talents with them—that of the arts and of very fine oratories. The music of the day was provided by professionals who had traveled the world over in their pursuits. Many of them performed at Radio City Music Hall and Carnegie Hall in New York City as well as the famous Chautauqua Institution in western New York just a few miles from the Cassadaga Lake Free Assembly. While performing at Chautauqua Institution, a setting of the arts, philosophy and religion, some performers were invited to the secret séances held in Laona, New York. Later they participated in séances and services in Lily Dale which led them to joining Spiritualism's ranks. For instance, Rev. Arthur Myers was a well-known actor on Broadway as well as a tenor singing in some of the most noted bands including the Paul Whitman Orchestra. His stage name was Arthur O'Mara. A few notes about Arthur. He was extremely protective of his voice and while he disliked any smoke or tobacco, he found a tad of bourbon soothed his throat. Also the Rev. Clyde Dibble, "the voice of Caruso"—loudly drifted down the veranda of the hotel from the music room on the corner. The Revs. Gladys and Kenneth Custance were world renowned harpists home-based in Onset, Massachusetts and Cassadaga, Florida.

As years passed, two very special Spiritualists became residents of the Cassadaga Camp. Arthur Myers had served as Postmaster at the Lily Dale Camp and then in Cassadaga, Florida for several years. He served tirelessly as a medium and orator. Spiritualism became his way of life. In fact, he was given the title "The Historian of Spiritualism." As manager of the hotel for several seasons, he enjoyed welcoming the northern guests and his many friends for the winter season. It was not uncommon to hear captivating piano music drifting from the Music Room, now the Gift Shop. And, best of all was listening to Arthur sing to his heart's content. Arthur loved being in the midst of things and found it convenient having his room on the first floor just off the side lobby. It not only kept him close to the Music Room but he could observe whatever was taking place on the first floor of the hotel.

Another beloved friend to all was the Rev. William Elliott Hammond, known by many as "Billy." He was a talented artist and his most notable portrait was "The Risen Christ." Billy was known as the "Dean of Modern Spiritualism" and also served well demonstrating his mediumship, teaching and oratories. It was not unusual to see a crowd around the veranda, sitting on the steps, railings, grass or standing as close as possible. It was either Arthur or Billy expounding on the philosophy of Spiritualism from just after the dinner hour to well beyond the midnight hour. Hammond, while oft times seemed so serious, displayed a unique sense of humor. He was very modest but did speak up asking that his middle initial 'E' be dropped and spelled out as Elliott to differentiate him from another with same initials of W. E. H. who was known to be a detriment to Spiritualism.

It is said that in 1875, the famed Emma Hardgine (Britten) predicted that Spiritualism would have three 50-year cycles—the first 50 years of physical phenomena from 1848-1898, following with the transitional period from 1898-1948, leaving the last 50-year cycle for mental mediumship from 1949-1999. This, in no way, meant that Spiritualism or its phenomena would end. She expressed that at the end of these three cycles, it would become known by many names. Then, it would move into its rightful place in the millennium—an age where spirituality would be sought by the multitudes and intuitive talent becoming a way of life. Certainly, its foundations had been solidly placed by Spiritualism's philosophy and the understanding of the Natural Law. Today in the Age of Aquarius, we are aware that this new century is quickly moving into a higher vibration. Time seems to be moving at a rapid pace. Séances are making a comeback as is physical phenomena.

Caesar Forman Healing Center

The Gazebo structure was moved from its original location just to the left of the entrance of the Colby Memorial Temple. It was remodeled in 1977. It was named the Caesar Forman Healing Center in recognition of the well-known and dedicated healer, Caesar Forman. For many years after his transition, one of the camp's residents, the Rev. Gladys Reid, held daily healing sessions. She gave freely of her time and talent.

CEASAR FORMAN HEALING CENTER

The Grand Ole Hotel

By 1903, the recently formed Cassadaga community had a need for the predominantly northern Spiritualists to reside during their seasonal stay. Emma Huff followed the Spirit message and was instrumental in having the construction of the original privately owned three-story wooden Cassadaga Hotel. They utilized the floor plan of the Maplewood Hotel in the sister camp at Cassadaga Lake Free Assembly in western New York as a guideline. It was constructed on Marion Street facing the lake.

ORIGINAL HOTEL 1903

The main entrance to the Camp was identified by the gate and gatehouse on the corner of Marion Street. In 1928 the entrance was moved to the corner of Stevens Street and S.R. 4139 with tall white-stone pillars on each side of Stevens Street. In 1940, larger white-stone pillars were installed.

STEVENS STREET ENTRANCE TODAY

In 1917 under the Florida Tax-Sale law, the ownership of the hotel and land was transferred to J. P. and Margaret McGill. The hotel continued to serve the registered guests for the Camp Winter Season and many that stayed until springtime. If one expected a stay, reservations had to be made two years in advance to be assured of a room. The hotel has always been the hub of the Community and meeting place for old and new friends, family and guests from all over the world. In the early years, it was first known as a haven for the northern Spiritualists.

For 23 years, the original Cassadaga Hotel had served the community very well. It met its fate on Christmas Eve of 1926 when it was demolished by a blazing fire. The fire is said to have occurred due to faulty electrical wiring on the second floor. It didn't go alone—the grocery story, pavilion and library each met its fate as well. Reconstruction of the hotel began almost immediately. Out of the ashes rose a two-story stucco Mediterranean architecture as seen today.

Edward F. Loud, Camp President, had the goal of making the Camp the greatest Spiritualist Assembly in the World. After the hotel was destroyed by the fire, he went about raising money for a new structure by selling bonds and collecting generous donations. In 1927, the concrete and fire-proof construction was completed as a 42-room two-story stone structure adorned on the west side of the first floor by the long veranda. The first season of 1927 celebrated the grand opening. It was extremely successful and Cassadaga, Florida was once again on the map as a winter resort for Spiritualists.

Mr. Loud also sought to reach his goal by having 3,000 linier feet of concrete sidewalks placed in the camp, more electric street lights, improved roads, store, bookshop, woman's club house and new properties on the lake. The residents helped by building 21 dwellings valued from $1,000 to $25,000. Although all this took place during Edward F. Loud's presidency, his legacy was the new hotel.

The camp was growing rapidly and necessitated an increase in the number of shares of stock available. Therefore,

Capital Stock Book 5, Page 26,
Paragraph 1(a), states, "Increase of Stock to $50,000 by creating an additional 2500 shares at $10.00 per share." Recorded 1928

During the hectic late 1920s and early 1930s the hotel was operated as a Stockholder Corporation known as the Cassadaga Hotel Company. It was under the directorship of William (Billy) Elliott Hammond. In the early 1930s due to the depression, financial difficulties made it impossible to pay the bonds. The Camp Board had no option but to sell the hotel.

In 1933, the Stow Foundation, an arm of the NSA became the new owner. It was managed by the Benevolent Society, an organization chartered by the NSA. The hotel was purchased with the idea of making it a home for retired ministers, healers and mediums. The baby grand piano continued to grace the music room and provide harmony to soothe the soul. A unique wooden antique phone booth with dial phone was the only phone and placed in the hotel lobby.

In 1934, the main advertisement for the Hotel Season read "Beautiful spacious parlors and lobby, cheerful airy dining room with seating for 150 guests, great food and high class service; 42 sleeping rooms with private or public baths, hot and cold running water in every room, beautifully furnished and equipped throughout, best heating system and a home for every guest."

Parks, Pagodas & Spirit Pond

The parks of yesterday such at Butler Park, Lake Park and Washington Park are gone. Recorded history failed to reveal what had taken place. They may now house various buildings or they may have been renamed. For many years through the 1980s, visitors came with picnic basket and blanket to enjoy a quiet spot among the grassy areas of the many parks and under the shade of the old moss-draped oak trees. In the late 1980s, Henry D. Smith, a paid groundskeeper, expanded the grounds availability by cutting deep into areas of high growth. New parks were named such as Harry Fogel Healing Park on Marion Street, Arthur Myers Park on Chauncey Street. Other parks as well continue to attract the visitors to the campgrounds, including Horseshoe Park, Medicine Wheel Park, Black Hawk Park, Seneca Park and Eloise Meditation Garden. Spiritualists have always loved to commune with nature. The chain of lakes of which Lake Colby is the nearest, offered opportunity for fishing, rowing and canoeing. While most of the activity on the lake was safe, it is known that two fishermen drowned in Spirit Pond in the 1950s. Today, due to the extreme drought in Florida, Spirit Pond is dry and Lake Colby is the size of a pond struggling to survive.

Mae Graves-Ward Gazebo

Seneca Park is one of the first parks in the camp. Today one can gaze lovingly at Seneca Park and the Gazebo that once overlooked the still-mirrored glassy Spirit Pond. It was one of nature's charming landscapes. It was not unusual to see an artist with easel, sketching the beauty of Cassadaga.

At the Annual Camp Meeting in March 29, 1986, a motion was made and passed by the membership that a suitable sign designate the Gazebo in Seneca Park as "The Mae Graves-Ward Gazebo" in honor and recognition of her untiring service to Spiritualism for more than 50 years. Mae received her certification as a Medium from the Indiana State Spiritualist Association. She was fortunate to have studied under the noted Dr. Victoria Barnes. Before moving to Cassadaga, Mae resided in Connecticut and soon became prominent for her talent as a Medium. For many years, she was one of the top three Mediums in the Cassadaga Camp.

Today, two statuesque cypress trees in front and on either side of the gazebo tower upward, proudly reaching toward the heavens. They began their journey as two seedlings. To the right of the gazebo is a Memorial placed in 1988 at the closing of the Celebration of Life Service for the famous Medium Mae Graves-Ward, known as the "Sophie Tucker of Spiritualism." The tree to the left is a Memorial placed in 1971 at the close of the Memorial

85

Service for the famous world-renowned Medium, Robert Bos—a natural medium who humbly served the poor and the rich alike. Later, another tree was placed by the family of the Rev. Helen Hanson in the grassy area northeast of the gazebo as a Memorial to her service to Spiritualism.

MAE GRAVES-WARD GAZEBO

Publications

In the early days of the Camp, news about Spiritualism around the country was available through *The Progressive Thinker*, Editor M. E. Cadwallader—*The Psychic Observer*, Editor Ralph Pressing—*Reason*, Editor A. B. Austin—*The Sunflower*, by the Sunflower Pub. Co., *Light of Truth* and *The Banner of Light*. The local newspaper of that day was entitled *The Cassadagan*, printed by the Deland News. In 1986, recognizing a need for and means of distributing news, a community monthly entitled *The Cassadagan* was reestablished under the Editorship of Marilyn J. Awtry. A short time thereafter, the Board of the Association sponsored a fly-sheet entitled *The Sunflower,* produced by the Camp Manager. As in days of old, the Board of Directors continues to publish an Annual Program. It becomes available in the early Fall of the year listing the scheduled events and provides information about the Camp. It is supported by advertisements in the program and by generous donations that are graciously accepted.

Men's and Women's Clubs

In the 1930s, the Community had two very active clubs—the Men's Club and the Cassadaga-Lake Helen Women's Club. They were both located outside of the Campgrounds. The Men's Club activities were held in the building across the street from the Camp on Cassadaga Road. The club had shuffle board teams, bowling leagues and a big brass band. Today this building is Brighid's Well, Inc. offering spiritual services as it did when previously known as the Universal Spiritual Centre founded by the late Rev. Ernie Sekuna.

In the early days, the Women's Club held their meetings in a large white house on Macy Street. It was chartered as "The Old and New Women's Club" and its motto was "Pure Aims, High Ideals and Unity of Purpose." Later the Camp Ladies Auxiliary was formed and met on the campgrounds in The Thatcher House on the corner of Palmer and Stevens Street. It was left to the Camp by the Last Will and Testament of Mrs. Thatcher. It faced the once peaceful waters of Spirit Pond. Many a fond memory remains of the happy times in that building. The sounds of laughter lingered after a full house at the Bingo Games on Saturday night or the women's card parties. As time passed the building became more of an activities building with the largest room established as the Camp Library. In the late 1960s, the Librarian was B. Anne Gehman. The interest in spirituality is on the rise today and many are seeking a path to follow. A library could once again be a major attraction to the Camp.

The Florida Spiritualist Association

One of the large houses constructed in the early days remains standing today on the corner of Seneca and Stevens Street just across from the Temple. It was the home of John and Charlotte Snipes who moved to Cassadaga from Massachusetts. They were extremely active in New England Spiritualist environment. After they purchased the wood-framed house in Cassadaga, they remodeled it into the magnificent structure that remains standing today. Many of the investigations of mediumship were conducted in the séance room in their home. After moving to Florida, John Snipes became President of the Florida Spiritualist Association, its office located in his house.

The County Courthouse Deed Book 257 Page 476 states "The Florida Spiritualist Association leased from SCSCMA 35 acres and all buildings for a term of 50 years from April 1, 1935 to March 31, 1985, County Courthouse Deed Book 257, Page 476."
Recorded March 30, 1935

The SCSCMA gave them a "Release of the Lease" as shown in Deed Book 259, Page 51.
Recorded April 11, 1935

In the late 1970s and 1980s it was owned and its beauty maintained by the Newcombs. Mr. Newcomb imported many of the exquisite furnishings from overseas. At Jane's transition, William Vavra inherited the house. A gateway entrance was constructed with an archway whose sign read Vavra's Villa.

From the Camp's inception, the Camp membership was made up of Spiritualists from various organizations including the Universal Spiritualists, National Spiritualists Association, Independent General Assembly, International Spiritualist Association, Universal Spiritualist Association and Universal Center of Psychic Science. The Reincorporation recorded September 29, 1986 changed the status to a closed camp. A closed camp does not allow for dual membership. Today there are open and closed camps throughout the United States.

Barber Shop

For a period of time, the Barber Shop was located in a cottage just across from the back of Harmony Hall on McKinley Street. Later, the cottage was designated as The Speaker's Cottage. It provided quarters for the medium and/or speaker to reside to fulfill their two-week contract during the Camp Season. In the latter part of 1970, the cottage became rental property and was for a number of years the residence of Rev. Harry and Mary Fogel. After Mary's transition, Harry became quite ill and was moved to High Springs, Florida where family could care for him. After he left the area, the Association sold the cottage and leased the land to the new owner.

Business Office

The Association has always maintained a business office. Several residents and longtime dedicated Spiritualists served as manager for a small gratuity. Records of the early days were not available but a few who served between 1960s through the 1980s were Duncan Beck, Jack Rutledge, Lois Marcet, John Weigl, Darleen Misskelly and Jonathan Ellis. The Association remains ever greatful to all who have served and those who are serving the Camp and Spiritualism today.

The Camp office has grown with the times and soon required a full-time salaried employee. Several times, the office was relocated within the Davis building. Up on the hill at 1325 Stevens Street was a very large home which served as the National Spiritualist Association of Churches General Headquarters. When the NSAC Board of Director's decided to move it to Lily Dale, New York in 1991, the building was put up for sale. The SCSCMA recognized it would nicely house its ever growing needs. The Camp purchased the property in 1993 and moved its office into the house. It is now named Summerland, a name created by Davis to represent the Spirit World. For many years, grounds keepers and maintenance men volunteered their time and labor.

SUMMERLAND—CAMP BUSINESS OFFICE

Governing Body

Every organization, whether profit or not-for-profit, requires a governing body to oversee the affairs of the organization. As a 501(c)3 church organization, it is especially important that knowledgeable members are nominated for positions on the Board of Directors. Not only must they understand the 501(c)3 non-profit laws but also understand the laws of the city, county, state and federal governments. At the annual meeting, the President Chairs the meeting, but the membership manages the affairs by motion, discussion and vote. Once the meeting draws to a close, it is the job of the Board of Directors to manage the affairs of the association as voted upon by the membership as well as handle any emergency issues that may arise.

The original incorporation document of the SCSCMA, as amended, set up that the governing body must be a seven person Board of Trustees. Election of Trustees takes place as established in the By-Laws at the Annual Meeting. Members in good standing may be nominated for the positions that have been vacated. Before accepting the nomination, the Chair should ask the question, "Do you understand that you have been nominated for a Volunteer Position?" This alleviates any problem arising after the election when the person is disappointed to find they do not get a pay check.

Since the SCSCMA has grown by leaps and bounds, it can no longer operate solely by volunteers. Therefore, employees are hired for specific part-time or full-time positions such as Camp Manager, Office Manager, Association Director, Bookstore Manager and staff, Grounds Maintenance and any other position necessary for an orderly operation of the Camp.

IX

The Changing Cassadaga Community

The Spiritualist philosophy teaches that we should strive to understand and practice the Natural Laws of the Universe. Spiritualists are aware of the Natural Law of Cycles and the Natural Law of Change—that is, what goes around comes around and nothing in the universe stays the same. Time has brought many changes to the Cassadaga Community.

Many of the old landmarks are gone. The Gatehouse and entrance to the Camp on the corner of Marion Street and Cassadaga Road is history. The entrance since 1940 has been graced with two large cement pillars at Stevens Street and Cassadaga Road. The large moss-draped trees stretching across Stevens Street created a tunnel-like atmosphere. Almost all of the aged moss-draped trees have returned to the earth from whence they came. Many of the houses and buildings of yesteryear no longer grace the land. Little by little the old times have drifted away as if into the world beyond. All of the dedicated Spiritualists who established and maintained the Camp as a "Spiritual Haven" for more than 70 years have graduated to the higher side of life. Others have simply moved on to new territory. Just as in yesteryear, Spiritualists as well as tourists still come to this special place that shares both sides of life.

DOWNTOWN CASSADAGA YESTERDAY

The hamlet was quite inviting with its lineup on the downtown main street—Mac Farland's Grocery Store, the U.S. Post Office, House of Charm Styling Salon, Novelty shop and the big round red and white sign identifying the Texaco Gas Station. In the late 1960s, the Gas Station faded out and the local Tavern became a reality. It provided a large dance floor in the rear of the building. In the 1980s, like many of the buildings, it was destroyed by fire. Throughout the years, the buildings along the strip have housed a variety of businesses including a realty company, beauty shop, gift shop, and a grocery store to meet the needs of the community. The downtown community buildings remain today although they have new owners and different types of businesses. The most noted change is the various types of readings offered by psychics, counselors, readers and a few mediums.

DOWNTOWN CASSADAGA TODAY

Cassadaga Community of yesterday was simply a quaint little town outside the gates of the Cassadaga Camp. Giant moss-draped trees were both inside and outside the gates surrounded by hills, ponds and lakes and many private homes. Today, downtown might be termed a small strip-mall. Although most of the tall moss-draped trees are gone, a few remain in this quaint and mystical hamlet known as Cassadaga, Florida.

DOWNTOWN CASSADAGA TODAY

Downtown Cassadaga is located at the intersection of Stevens Street and Cassadaga Road. On the corners of the intersection stand the United States Post Office, the Andrew Jackson Davis Building and the grand Historic Cassadaga Hotel. The U.S. Post Office is a place where the residents meet in passing and catch up on the latest local news. It is a tiny building but offers full and courteous service. Tourists loved to send off a card with the hand stamp of "Cassadaga Florida."

Today, the Cassadaga Community includes:

BRIGHID'S WELL

(Previously the Universal Spiritual Center)
Driving east on S.R. 4139 just over the hill, the newly painted building at 460 Cassadaga Road reaches out to you. Long ago, it housed the Men's Club and through the years served as the home of several churches. Since 1972, it has been family-owned and the home of the Universal

Spiritual Centre founded by Dr. Ernie Sekuna. After his transition, the Center continued under the ownership of his son, Matthew Sekuna.

Matt continues to manage Omni Orion, Inc., which offers for sale metaphysical gifts and development tools. The Universal Center itself is still family-owned but has been turned over to his partner, Cynthia Botsko. She has reincarnated the Center as *Brighid's Well, Inc.* It is nestled under the shade of the old oak trees beckoning the seekers of today a cheery "Welcome."

Brighid's Well is not only a book store and gift shop. It offers educational opportunities and gatherings for healing and meditation. Classes are available for your enlightenment as you travel your pathway of life. Several types of Intuitive Readings and Mediumship are available. A well-stocked Book Store and Gift Shop provide a variety of items pleasing to the eye and the mind. Its doors are always open offering a genuine welcome to the public.

THE PURPLE ROSE OF CASSADAGA

The Purple Rose Trading Company was opened by June and Fred Bowermaster in 1985 at 1079 Stevens Street. The shop was geared to be a "Buy, Sell and Trade" shop. As said by June, "...Then, one day we finally decided what we wanted to be—it's to be a friendly place where one can be welcomed with not only a smile but *a big hello* and where the customers can have their questions answered appropriately."

The shop carries jewelry, stones, crystals, Native American Indian items, spiritual and metaphysical items. Spiritual readers are also available.

Today, June is a part of the shop in Spirit as she has moved on to the higher life. The shop is under the management of her granddaughter C. Green. She has assembled a wide variety of goods in the store. Green also expanded the shop to the outside world with an on-line store.

Readers are available daily. A comfy sitting area, sheltered from the sun, is made available to guests awaiting a session. As always, you are welcome!

THE HISTORIC CASSADAGA HOTEL
In 1979, the NSAC sold the hotel. Three months later it was sold again to the new owners John and Diana Morn. For several years management was under the direction of John and Lollie Weigl. Later, the Morn's leased it to be transformed into a registered nursing facility. In the late 1980s, it was reestablished as a hotel and managed by Joe Stuper assisted by Henry D. Smith. The long Veranda became active once again. Room No. 3 housed Irene's Antique Shop. The other rooms on the veranda were occupied by registered mediums from

various Spiritualist organizations. The first weekend of every month guests came from near and far to receive a healing session with the world famous Bill Clark, known as "The Man with Healing Hands." The yearly arrival of mediums from England, Ray and Maureen Jones, was long awaited by the many who sign up for private sessions. The ground level side entrance welcomed one to the well-kept rose garden leading to the Rose Garden Gifts, Books, and Things—Henry D. Smith, proprietor.

CASSADAGA HOTEL 1980

In June 1992, John and Diana assumed the management of the hotel and renovated it. The Lobby welcomed one to a comforting spirit vibration, a variety of free literature, flyers and activity programs in Cassadaga and around the country. The rooms were tastefully redecorated and the quiet solitude was welcoming. The Lost in

Time Café offered visitors a pleasing variety of foods. The Banquet Hall (once the restaurant) was remodeled and renamed Seneca Hall. A gift shop became available as well. At that time, the Spiritual Center was chartered by Universal Spiritualist Association of Nevada and periodically offered seminars and classes. Then in 1999, a disturbing energy surrounded the area as a large "For Sale" sign was posted. It was short lived. The owners had a change of heart and took down the sign.

Today both the main and side lobby offer lovely comfortable furnishings reminding one of days of old. The Gift Gallery has a variety of gifts, jewelry, precious stones, candles and incense, a wide variety of Native American articles, books, the exact gift you want for that special person and other treasures. Many items are hand-designed by local artisans. The shop is managed by Diana Morn.

Various types of readers, psychics and a few mediums are available seven days a week by appointment or walk-in. There are special activities such as Spiritual Development Classes, Meditation Circles, various modalities of healing and Shamanic Rituals for the purpose of enriching and transforming your life.

The hotel rooms are neat and welcoming taking you back in time. Since there are neither telephones nor television in the rooms, you will find peace, peace, heavenly peace.

It is suggested you make reservations as rooms are often booked well in advance of activities. Visiting Cassadaga offers you the opportunity to stroll amidst nature and relax on the hotel veranda.

CASSADAGA HOTEL TODAY

The Cassadaga Hotel has recently been registered as a Historical Landmark. Today, many new things are on the horizon.

The Lost in Time Café has been replaced by Sinatra's Ristorante' which offers an authentic Italian menu. The restaurant is nestled on the main floor of the enchanting Cassadaga Hotel. During dinner on Friday and Saturday evenings live music can be enjoyed played on a restored white-maple baby grand piano circa mid-1800s and is one of the original pieces in the hotel. The main dining room hosted many gatherings in the years past and continues to do so today. The Sunday afternoon dinner has been replaced with a home-cooked brunch served from 9 a.m. until 2 p.m.

The wicker rockers of yesterday, once on the grand veranda, have been replaced with new furnishings offering a place to sit and gaze at the old-world charm of the town of Cassadaga.

THE PSYCHIC THERAPY CENTER

The Cassadaga Psychic Therapy Center has made its home for many years just behind the Post Office on the corner of Macy and S.R. 4139. It was founded by Bill Hermann. He held unfoldment classes and provided readings right up to the time of his passing.

Today, the Center is operated by family members. The belief expounded upon by their Cassadaga Spiritualist Church is that there are a variety of paths available today and although this causes confusion, it should not bring despair. Rather it should lead one to look deeper into the presence that motivates and challenges one to seek what is beyond our understanding—to look for the essence of life. The Center welcomes you.

As we step inside the gates of the Spiritualist Camp we find

THE CHANGING
SOUTHERN CASSADAGA SPIRITUALIST
CAMP MEETING ASSOCIATION

The fence no longer surrounds the Association's grounds, although rusted segments may be found on some of its borders. Buildings remaining from the past are Brigham Hall and Harmony Hall with rental apartments upstairs and offices of mediums downstairs, the Colby Memorial Temple and the Andrew Jackson Davis Building.

In 1917, the Southern Cassadaga Spiritualist Camp Meeting Association joined organized Spiritualism under the umbrella of the NSA. In 1981, the Board of the SCSCMA returned the charter and became an independent entity. In 1986, it was recognized that the Corporation was just years away from coming to a close. The Board of the Association chose to change the status of the SCSCMA by filing a Reincorporation document in Tallahassee, Florida September 29, 1986. In April 1990, it registered with the Internal Revenue Service as a Church Corporation. Today, as a church corporation, it is confined to its own membership and rules. Like many camps it is listed as an Independent Camp and no longer has open membership. Several of the Spiritualist Camps today are closed membership. That simply means they have filed for their own Incorporation and have a Constitution and By-Laws to meet their needs. They also set up their own educational standards, classes and certification programs.

Although the status has changed, the invitation to the general public remains open to all of its activities. It is no longer a seasonal camp but rather continues to hold meetings for the advancement of knowledge by offering classes, seminars and workshops year round. It offers the seeker a large variety of opportunities to learn about Spiritualism—a Science, Philosophy and Religion.

The guiding principle of the Camp is The Golden Rule and the beliefs are based on Natural Law, the continuity of life, spiritual enlightenment and spiritual healing. The Book Store and Gift Shop offer books to educate and elevate the soul.

Unlike days of old, guided walking tours are available to you where you may hear some things you always wanted to know or learn of the energy fields where spirit photography may be at its best.

The Sunday afternoon Church Service is now held in the morning hour with the addition of a luncheon in the Andrew Jackson Davis building. A one-hour all message service by students and certified mediums follows the luncheon.

Just as in days of old, the Cassadaga Spiritualist Camp Program booklet is made available annually providing a complete insight into the Camp and all of its activities.

NATIONAL HISTORIC REGISTER

The National Register requires filing of a registration form which provides a physical description of the place, information on its history and significance and a bibliography. The Camp filed the form and was accepted as a place worthy of preservation. On March 14, 1992, the Southern Cassadaga Spiritualist Camp Meeting Association was accepted and is listed in the National Historical Register.

TRANSFER OF PROPERTY

The Warranty Deed Book, Page 491, File 836 records a transfer of land from the Southern Cassadaga Spiritualist Camp Meeting Association to the County of Volusia, State of Florida stating "...property in descriptive terms as part of Lot 1 Section 5, Township 18 South, Range 31 East. The title hereby conveyed is contingent expressly upon the County of Volusia improving, beautifying and draining the property here conveyed and the maintenance upon said property of a public park." It further stipulated "that if the County failed to complete improvements and maintain it exclusively as a public park and play ground, it would revert to the SCSCMA."
Recorded February 5,1940
Signed by William Elliott Hammond, President and Edgar D. Eldridge, Secretary.

That park has been maintained by the county since the date of transfer. Today, it also provides an entrance to Colby-Alderman Park.

COLBY-ALDERMAN PARK

A new addition to the area adjacent to the park maintained by Volusia County is the 124-acre park—a new project funded by Volusia County ECHO grant program. It can also be entered at 1099 Massachusetts Avenue. George Colby sold his property to his friends. Their grandson, William Amory Underhill, a noted attorney who formerly served as U.S. Attorney General of the United States donated this and adjoining land as a memorial of his grandparents. Enjoy both the paved and unpaved trails, stopping to read all the many glassed informational signs and learn its interesting history. You can walk the trail crossing over the ground where George P. Colby made his first home in Florida. Although the large orange grove is gone, a few trees remain and still bear fruit. Following the trail to the fenced platform, view the scenery Colby viewed from his front porch. Unfortunately due to the drought, the large Lake Colby of yesterday is now a small pond.

BANANA GROVE

PARK

PAVILION

THE ORIGINAL ORANGE GROVE TODAY

WALKWAY

A NEW AGE ON THE HORIZON

The changes of the times are always noticeable. Downtown Cassadaga's focal point is the U. S. Post Office, accompanied by the Cassadaga Hotel, The Purple Rose and the white stone gateposts leading into the Southern Cassadaga Spiritualist Camp Meeting Association.

The SCSCMA continues today under its own guidelines and rules. Its predominant requirement is that no tools of any kind may be utilized in the demonstration of mediumship. Others in the Cassadaga community practice a variety of modalities including Astrology, Counseling, Handwriting Analysis, Palmistry, Past Life Regressions, Planchette and Tarot Card Readings.

The question is often asked why these modalities are not practiced in the Cassadaga Spiritualist Camp. The reason is that, although modalities may be very accurate or may be offered by psychics, they "do not prove the continuity of life" and that is the primary requirement of Mediumship.

Human beings on earth are spirit clothed in a physical body. Once the spirit discards the physical body, the mind energy continues on in the Spirit World. It is important to understand the differences in a psychic and a medium.

✎ A mediums is one whose organism is sensitive to the vibrations from the spirit world—therefore they receive communication from a spirit entity (one who once lived on earth) to pass on to the sitter. A medium does not need to ask questions, carry on a dialogue with the sitter, or interpret the message; they simply give you what they are told by the Spirit. Spiritualist mediums are dedicated to demonstrating proof of the continuity of life by communication with the Spirit World. Since everyone is capable of working on a psychic level, a medium may also be a psychic. Thus, some use the term medium-psychic.

✎ A psychic is able to link with universal knowledge and/or with the aura of the sitter and using logic translates that which they glean to the sitter. Extra-sensory perception also plays a part in psychism. The message is usually about mundane affairs such a livelihood, relationships and the future.

It is possible for a medium to be a psychic but a psychic is not a medium. Since the other modalities mentioned do not prove the continuity of life, they are not a part of the Spiritualist Camp. Spiritualism encourages practice of the Natural Law. The Law of Tolerance affords one the opportunity to be tolerant and respectful of the belief system of others. Each is in their rightful place at this moment in time!

Mediumship is identified under the Science of Spiritualism. In this fast changing world, the workers in the vineyard of Spiritualism must uphold the Science, Philosophy and Religion of Modern Spiritualism always remembering that

> As the Sunflower turns its face
> To the Light of the Sun
> So Spiritualism turns the face of humanity
> To the Light of Truth.

X

Then There Was George

After the Southern Cassadaga Spiritualist Camp Meeting Association was up and running, it is recorded Colby served the Camp periodically for several years. Little is documented of his life but is has been recorded that during his 19th year he chose to repudiate his family religion and left the church. It was then that he began his public work as a medium and traveled from one place to another giving private sessions or séances. Many articles in various Spiritualist magazines state that he went north for the summer season and served in Camps and churches across the United States. George's services were always desired for he was a *good test medium* and a *well-informed trance speaker.*

The bound minutes of the formulative Convention of September 1893 establishes that Colby was nominated and ran for a position on its Board. By a unanimous vote, he became a Trustee. Just three months later on December 19, 1893, a letter bearing Colby's signature, was written to Robert Dimmick, Secretary of the NSA, stating "I wish to say I am not a member of that Association, and my name was placed there without my knowledge or consent. Its further use in this connection, is hereby forbidden... . A letter in the files explains this erratic behavior. George was very ill and spent several months convalescing in the home of Spiritualists in Washington, D.C.

In 1925, at age 77, after 25 years of absence, Colby visited the Lily Dale Assembly in New York. Upon his return to Florida, things did not go well for George and he became financially strapped. His business empire was gone and he was not at all physically well. Once again, George became disenchanted with the local Spiritualists and he sold his home on the shores of Lake Colby in Cassadaga and moved to New Smyrna Beach. After several years the house was abandoned and fell into horrible disrepair. Later it met its fate with fire.

Although he disassociated himself with Spiritualists and had quit the National Spiritualist Association in December of 1893, the Stow Benevolent Society of the NSA/NSAC provided George with a gratuity every month of his life. It appears George had a change of heart. On December 21, 1931, George wrote to the secretary of the NSA saying, "I cannot tell you in words the feeling of gratitude I owe you and the NSA Board for the help the pension has been to me... ." One of the young men he had raised also assisted in his care for many years.

In 1929, at age 81, Colby was without funds and somewhat disabled. He was brought back to the Cassadaga Camp. For his birthday in January, his remaining friends at the camp provided him with baskets of food and cash. The SCSCMA provided him with an apartment in Harmony Hall for a very short time. Colby was on the decline and really not able to care for himself. The U.S. Summer Census of 1930 confirms his residency with Mr. Edwin and Mrs. Alice M. Spencer of Lake Helen. They took care of his every need for three years. As George became very feeble and ill it was obvious that he required hospitalization. The Spencers took him to the County Home and he was placed in a Hospital Unit in Deland. The County Records Volume 589, Page 11341 records "George Colby, male, white; no money, needed for his care." His stay there was cut short. The Superintendent of the Home notified the National Spiritualist Association by letter that on the morning of July 17, 1933 a stroke had paralyzed George leaving him unable to have use of his right side. He had lost most of his ability to speak. This final illness opened the doorway for George Prescott Colby's graduation to the Spirit World on Tuesday, July 27, 1933.

Once again, many stories have been repeated over the years. One story is that Colby's physical remains were interred in Lake Helen-Cassadaga Cemetery. Others state his body was flown back to his northern haven. Neither appears to be true.

Official documents state that the Rev. William "Billy" Elliott Hammond, a long time friend of George and resident of Cassadaga, made a strong plea and rallied the Camp Board and the camp residents "to dig deep into their pockets and raise the money so that arrangements could be made to take care of the remains of their dear friend and neighbor, George P. Colby." The plea was successful. Hammond made the arrangements for George's physical remains to be cremated and his ashes sent north for interment. After that was accomplished, Hammond reported funds remained from the generosity of his friends and neighbors in the both the Cassadaga Spiritualist Camp and in Lake Helen.

Hammond queried the Camp Board at that time to receive approval to place a stone in Colby's honor on the campgrounds. The Board denied the request stating it may set a precedent for future requests. Hammond turned to the authorities of the Lake Helen-Cassadaga Cemetery. They were in agreement that a tombstone should be placed in his honor and memory in the Lake Helen-Cassadaga Cemetery near the community George P. Colby homesteaded and loved so very much—the hamlet he named Cassadaga, Florida. The tombstone is in the Cemetery but George's remains are not. On May 17, 2013, an official probe by Lake Helen Cemetery authorities was carried out on Plot #12. The attendant tested the depth back and forth across the grave and up and down from tombstone to bottom of the plot. It revealed the plot is empty, thus supporting the records that Hammond had his remains cremated and returned to New York. There is another type of test that can be done at the gravesite but it is extremely costly. Research continues seeking details from the funeral home and crematory engaged in 1933. Future writings may reveal the findings.

It has been said by a source considered reliable that Colby's ashes were returned to Lily Dale and a friend placed them under a stone marker around "The Stump." This is a logical theory. It is well-known that Colby demonstrated his mediumship standing proudly on The Stump at many of the afternoon services. The Stump is the base of a huge tree that once towered high reaching toward the sky. A deadly storm in the early years of the Camp downed the tree. Later, to protect the stump, it was covered in cement. Three steps lead to this new platform. Mediums would stand on the platform and give messages from the Spirit World to the large crowds. No longer can one stand on the Stump. The cement Stump is now very delicate from age and weather. It is protected by a gated fence encircling it. Today, two all-message services are offered for the numerous guests that attend the Lily Dale Assembly during their summer season.

As to George Colby's ashes—will we ever know if they were actually placed under one of the stones around the Stump? Some stones do have a name carved, in a fashion, but many are void of identification. Colby's name has not been found on any of them. If his ashes were placed there in 1933, it is doubtful that the person (probably Hammond) handling it is still on the earth plane but rather is in the higher side of life. There is no doubt that Hammond and Colby are having a laugh over the mystery.

GEORGE COLBY'S TOMBSTONE

XI

Spiritualist Camps and Organizations Today

From Modern Spiritualism's beginning in 1848, it grew by leaps and bounds reaching millions. Then it had a severe decline but due to the many lives that were lost in World War I, Spiritualism's adherents increased. Many wanted to hear from their loved ones whose lives had been cut short. Because of Spirit communication and receiving a message that settled their mind, large numbers turned to Spiritualism's philosophy and soon joined its ranks. The great need of and pressure on mediums to accommodate the masses at that time, caused fraudulent mediumship to become a serious problem. These so-called mediums were brought to trial and sentenced to insane asylums or jails. It took many years for Spiritualism to erase that stain and re-establish itself. Truth always prevails!

Once again in the 1980s and 1990s, Spiritualism's numbers vacillated. When the 21st Century entered, it brought the knowledge that the Aquarian Age would usher in a major positive changing factor for Spiritualism as a Science, Philosophy and Religion. This Century is the one that declares doing away with the old—Materialism and bringing in the new—Spirituality. With this being the major force in this Age, Spiritualism's numbers are already on the upward trend. The re-appearance of the Home Circle and dedication by individuals to unfold their innate abilities brings with it a rise in membership. Another factor is the revival of the science of Spiritualism. In the second decade of this century, physical phenomena are becoming evident once again and scientific investigation needs to step up to the plate. Delegates assembled in Convention in 2011 voted to establish a committee to help in re-establishing the Science. Positive results were reported in the 2012 Convention. All Spiritualist organizations should consider setting aside the second Sunday in August to celebrate "Science Day." It is suggested that a special oratory and offering be taken to provide funding necessary for continuing investigation of the phenomena of Spiritualism in this 21st Century.

As more and more individuals seek to find themselves, they are also recognizing that all of humanity has intuitive ability within their being. This Century brings the Age of Spirituality and the unfolding of one's intuitive nature. We are moving into a more refined vibration—one of oneness and awareness.

Now is the time for Spiritualism to take its rightful place as a Science, Philosophy and Religion. Spiritualism will once again rise to new heights.

SPIRITUALISM'S CAMPS TODAY

Today, there are a total of 21 Spiritualist Camps; eight are Independent and 13 chartered by the NSAC as follows:

INDEPENDENT SPIRITUALIST CAMPS

Arizona
Sun Spiritualist Camp

California
Harmony Grove Spiritualist Camp

On May 16, 2014, a raging fire severely affected Escondido, California. It destroyed the century old Harmony Grove Spiritualist Association's camp. Out of the 30 homes on the campgrounds, 24 homes and four church buildings were left in ashes. The Board has already begun to plan rebuilding the Camp. Spiritualists throughout the United States are offering prayers and financial assistance. It will be wonderful to see Harmony Grove Camp's grand reopening.

Florida
So. Casssadaga Spiritualist Camp Meeting Association

Indiana
Chesterfield Spiritualist Camp

Kansas
Sunset Spiritualist Camp

Maine
Etna Spiritualist Camp

Massachusetts
Lake Pleasant Spiritualist Camp

Michigan
Snowflake Spiritualist Camps

CHARTERED SPIRITUALIST CAMPS (NSAC)

Connecticut
Pine Grove Spiritualist Camp

Illinois
Cherry Valley Spiritualist Camp

Iowa
Mississippi Valley Spiritualist Association

Maine
Madison Spiritualist Camp Meeting Association

Pinpoint Spiritualist Camp

Temple Heights

Massachusetts
On-I-Set Wigwam Spiritualist Camp

Michigan
Northern Lake Michigan Spiritualist Camp

Minnesota
Chain Lake Spiritualist Camp

New York
Lily Dale Assembly

Ohio
Ashley Spiritualist Camp

Washington
Camp Edgewood

Wisconsin
Western Spiritualist Camp Association (Wonewoc)

MAJOR SPIRITUALIST ORGANIZATIONS TODAY

UNITED STATES

There are 13 major organizations functioning in the United States at the present time. The alphabetical list follows.

American Federation of Spiritualists (AFS)
Fellowship of the Spirit (FOTS)
General Assembly of Spiritualists (G.A.S.)
Harmonial Philosophy Association (HPA)
Independent Spiritualist Association of USA (ISA)
International General Assembly of Spiritualists (IGAS)
National Spiritualist Association of Churches (NSAC)
So. Cassadaga Spiritualist Camp
Meeting Assoc. (SCSCMA)
The National Spiritualist Alliance (TNSA)
Universal Church of the Masters (UCM)
United Spiritualist Church Association (USCA)
Universal Harmony Foundation (UHF)
Universal Spiritualists Association (USA)

The total number of Spiritualist Churches in the United States is unknown as there has not been a Spiritualist Census in more than 100 years. Current directories vary and many are not up-to-date.

ENGLAND (UK)

The primary organization in England is The Spiritual National Union. It is based in London and is the largest Spiritualist organization in the world. It also has three churches within the United States.

The Greater World Christian Spiritualist Association (GWCSA) was founded in 1931 as the Greater World Christian and Spiritualist League. It has 60 churches in the UK and in several other countries.

INTERNATIONAL SPIRITUALIST FEDERATION (ISF)

The International Spiritualist Federation headquarters is in the United Kingdom. The membership is made up of Spiritualist organizations and individual Spiritualists from around the world.

Spiritualism stands at the crossroads. All of the individual organizations are in agreement that their foundation is based on "the truth of the continuity of life by means of Spirit communication." They know there is strength in unity. If Spiritualists of today desire to fulfill the dream of our Pioneers—Spiritualism, the Light of the World—it is time to unite in oneness of being and purpose.

XII

Cassadaga and
The 21ˢᵗ Century

Although some of today's media have presented Cassadaga in a positive vein, it is time that the guessing game ends and those outside of its boundaries become aware of what the Cassadaga Community is really all about.

Cassadaga, just like in the days gone by, is not a strange mystical town of the occult. There are no cult leaders, no gypsies, no crystal balls, nor turbans. There are no witches and no warlocks. There are just residents like that of any community—simply normal people. Within that community is the Southern Cassadaga Spiritualist Camp Meeting Association often referred to simply as the Cassadaga Spiritualist Camp or Cassadaga Camp. It is the home of Spiritualists who guide their lives by the Declaration of Principles of Spiritualism and the Natural Laws. Many are drawn to live in the community to be with like-minded folks, to study and unfold their innate ability as mediums and healers as well as stimulate their psyches. Others come who already have certification.

The Cassadaga community just happens to be a quiet hamlet off unto itself in the midst of the hills, lakes, ponds and woodlands of Volusia County. It is a community welcoming all those who choose to enter therein. As within the entire universe, Spirits wander freely in and outside of the community. Spirits—Yes; Ghosts—No.

All of the pioneers that once lived within the confines of the Cassadaga Spiritualist Camp have made their transition to the Spirit World. Most of the torchbearers that carried on through the years have also moved to the higher side of life—a very few remain. Those that have moved on into higher realms of life continue to grow and can communicate with those who are on the earth plane. Spirits that have elevated themselves in the Spirit World are free to travel whenever and wherever they choose. Yes, they may visit once in a while, but they do not linger on the lower planes of life for they live in a continued phase of progression. They have completed their earth-life experience.

Mediums and mediumship are a very important part of the science of Spiritualism. To be a good professional Medium, it takes a lot of time spent in self-growth and soul-growth. Without that, the medium has difficulty in attuning to Spirit. Those desiring to unfold their inherent abilities and become certified mediums as well as commissioned healers must elevate their soul level in order to attract the best communicators and healers from the higher side of life. This is accomplished by the medium making it a daily practice to sit in the silence as well as practice meditation. In communication with Spirit, the medium raises the consciousness to a higher vibration and the spirit lowers its vibration so the two can make a clear contact.

It should be noted that the term "medium" was created in the mid-1800s. In today's world the terminology conducive to describing one who can make contact with the spirit world has many options such as Medium, Spirit Communicator, Spirit Intermediary, Clairvoyant, Channel and Reader. Spiritual and Evolutionary Counselor are accepted as well.

Today, the camp can be said to be basically a new generation of Spiritualists carrying forth the torch of its predecessors.

The Cassadaga Community is:

- ☞ A Community of everyday people from all walks of life.

☞ A Community where Spiritualists live both inside and outside of the Camp and practice their intuitive nature under credentials of Mediumship, Healers, Teachers and Ministers from various Spiritualist organizations.

☞ A Community that has a Spiritualist Camp. Those Mediums and Healers within the confines of the Camp have gone through an Educational Program set up by the Camp and served diligently as students before being credentialed by vote of the Board of Directors.

☞ A Church within the Southern Cassadaga Spiritualist Camp Meeting Association that is within its own boundaries with its own Constitution and By-laws by which to abide. It meets in the Colby Memorial Temple.

☞ A community with a hotel—the Cassadaga Hotel providing cozy rooms for its guests—a Bookstore and Gift Shop—Psychics and Mediums. It also offers Sinatra's Restaurant providing full service, delicious food and soothing music for the soul.

☞ A Community that opens its doors to business entrepreneurs.

☞ A Community that opens its doors to Mediums, Psychics, Readers and Counselors from other towns who come to do an honest day's work. And just like other communities, the work force consists of varied talents such as Postal employees, waitresses, food preparers, bar tenders, sales clerks, cashiers, gift and book store managers and varied maintenance trades. Many are talented in the arts and others in professions requiring college degrees. They, too, choose to be a part of this community. They often join in the classes that are available.

☞ A community that has learned to practice the Natural Law of Tolerance. Many people in this community have various religious beliefs. Spiritualists within this community are guided by the Declaration of Principles and taught to practice the Natural Law in daily living. In its religious belief system, Spiritualists practice varied mediumistic, psychic and healing techniques. These folks realize everyone is in their rightful place and have the freedom of the Natural Law of Choice.

☞ A Community that opens its doors to seekers of truth.

☞ A Community that welcomes You!

As time passes by, we are assured that the Natural Law of the universe will continue to prevail—we know it to be immutable and always operating the same way under the same conditions. Natural Law assures us that the future will bring more changes for "life goes on—here and hereafter."

ALL of this makes up what is known today as nostalgic Cassadaga, Florida—a small hamlet in the rolling hills and lakes, awaiting its own destiny!

A toast of the past is shared again today in a poem written by H. B. Locklaw in 1929.

Cassadaga, the Beautiful

Of the beauty of Cassadaga,
I need not speak to those
Who have dwelt within her borders,
And plucked the lovely rose
That grows along the roadside,
And in the garden where
A gentle hand hath waterfed,
And hath tendered it with care.

Then all the little wild flowers,
Around each bush and tree—
Where host of birds are singing,
Their songs of merry glee.

The fragrance of the orange blooms
That greet one everywhere
Fills all the air with sweetness
Naught can with them compare.

The people are so wonderful,
They are here for rest and health,
They are like one big family
They like not thought of wealth.
They are genial, kind to everyone
With a hand held out to all—
You'll meet them at the tea parties,
At card parties and the ball.

There are lecturers for all who wish
To steal a while from care,
And listen to what the preacher says
And join with him in prayer.
We Welcome all to join our band
For work as well as play,
To listen to the Bluebirds song
And to the good old northern blue jay.

The whippoorwill is calling
In notes so loud and clear—
Oh! Come to Cassadaga,
We need you here this Year!

Although this poem can be modified based on the changes that have occurred down through the years, one thing remains steadfast—that is,

Cassadaga, Florida Welcomes You!

EVANS RESIDENCE

AWTRY RESIDENCE

BURLEY RESIDENCE

CHIRNSIDE RESIDENCE

RESIDENCE

APPENDICES

Appendix A

Tribute to George P. Colby

This undated handwritten document by Harrison D. Barrett, the first President of the National Spiritualist Association (NSA) was prepared by request for placement in one of the Spiritualist newspapers of the day. It casts light on the life and actions of George Prescott Colby.

A TRIBUTE TO GEORGE P. COLBY

"The illness of Bro. Geo. P. Colby, the eminent lecturer and test medium of Lake Helen, Florida has been mentioned before in the columns of your excellent paper. Mr. Colby is well-known to the writer whose privilege it has been to catch glimpses of his past life from those who knew him best in the earlier years of his life. It is now more than thirty years since he became aware of his mediumship. During all that time despite the strenuous opposition from nearest relatives and friends, he has never faltered in his outspoken loyalty to the cause of

Spiritualism and his voice has been raised in its behalf in places where his life might have been forfeited had it not been for his own indomitable courage and the assistance of the arisen loved ones who protected him from harm. He has spoken in places where angry mobs have threatened violence to his person yet, sustained by his unseen force he went bravely on with his work and the earnestness of his own soul has won him many a victory where people with less confidence in the Spirit World would have suffered harm.

On not a few occasions, he has been sought by men of desperate character with the intention of removing him from this locality because of his communion with spirits. But in every instance, Bro. Colby with the assistance of his guide, Seneca, has succeeded in conquering their fierce natures and sent them from him with tearful eyes and prayerful hearts. He has carried the torch of Spiritualism in all of its brilliancy into places shrouded by the darkest gloom of orthodox bigotry and superstition and illuminated them with pure white light of truth. He was early imbued with the missionary spirit and sought by way means in his power to instruct the people from the mine of knowledge furnished him by the spirit philosopher Seneca.

All through the early years of his mediumship, Bro. Colby gave freely of his treasures feeling that he should not accept pay for the gifts of the Spirit. The people of that day were not educated in the ethics of giving but were willing to receive something for nothing; hence permitted our friend to toil on unrequited for his arduous labor.

GEORGE PRESCOTT COLBY

He had a message for the people and went forth regardless of the cost to himself to give it to them. Had he heeded the voice of the guides on all occasions, he might have been spared such suffering by charging for his services but his generous nature could not then see the necessity of doing so; hence he continued his labors of love neither asking nor receiving remuneration for his toil. It would occupy too much of your space to give an account in detail of the earlier years of his mediumship. Appointments were made for him far and wide, and he set out to fill them to the very letter. So poorly was he paid at times that he couldn't afford to travel either by rail or stage, hence had to go on foot on many a journey from one town to another. Indeed, this was not all. In order to save his clothing, he would on leaving one village remove his shoes and stockings and walk barefooted until he came in sight of the next town where he was to speak when he would put them on again. This was a necessity, fellow Spiritualists, for his compensation was too small to permit him to purchase even articles of ordinary comfort and he was forced to be thus extravagantly economical.

His spiritual unfoldment was rapid and his mediumship became second to none in its power and absolute genuineness. Those who have had the blessed privilege of listening to the poetic philosophy of Seneca and heard his wonderful word paintings can attest to the beauty of this man's remarkable mediumship. It is almost worth a life of pain and suffering to have for a companion in Spirit such a one as Seneca. But there should be some compensation for our spiritual martyrs here on earth for Bro. Colby is not the only one of our workers who has been compelled to suffer through the thoughtless selfishness of our Spiritualist friends. Yet how can they receive it unless the people are brought to a clearer recognition of the philanthropic side of Spiritualism are embodied in the axiom 'things equal to the same things are equal to each other.' In other words our speakers and mediums should receive just compensation for labor. Bro. Colby has always been delicate in health from his boyhood and the severe strain put on his physical during the years of his tenacity soon sent him upon a sick bed. Indeed he was often prostrated by illness during those years of unremitting toil. About eight years ago, it seemed as if the sands of his young life were running low and that he was about to enter the 'great unseen' of which he had given so many beautiful pictures to the sorrowing mortals of earth. His guide took the matter in hand and advised him to remove to Florida. He did so and has dwelt in that fair land of flowers for nearly a score of years. His health improved perceptibly in that sunny clime but the vigor of strength never came back to him.

He took up some Government land and prepared to make himself a home there. Small farming and orange growing seemed to give fair prospects of a just return for his labor when it was found that he was not equal to severe manual labor, even with the improved state of his health. Still he did what he could working alone and living alone. A hermit's life may have its enchantments for some men but to a sensitive—a medium, it becomes torture sometimes because of the impulse to do for others that the Spirit would always lay upon its instrument. 'Obedient to the heavenly vision or voice of the spirit guides,' he attended to his little farm and did what he could for Spiritualism in his immediate neighborhood. He placed Spiritualism in a most favorable light before the people of Florida and made their minds receptive to its divine beliefs. During the past eighteen years he has frequently visited the northern states during the summer season but with every approach of winter he has been forced to return to his home in the sunny south. He has spoken in every state and territory in the union with the exception of six or eight and wherever he has gone he has left hosts of warm friends behind. In California, Oregon, Washington and British Columbia, his work was very remarkable. His friends here speak in the highest terms of him as a man and refer to his visit as the leading event in the history of Spiritualism in their localities.

Last winter, he was the central figure among the speakers at the Camp Meeting in De Leon Springs, Florida where he made many warm friends through whose influence he secured Camp engagements in the north during the past season. Wherever he went from Lake Brady to Onset Bay, he left many friends to regret his departure and to look forward to his promised return next year. When the Camp Season closed, he went to

Chicago to attend the National Convention as a delegate from a Society in Florida. On the floor of the Convention he became an earnest worker and was made a member of a number of important committees. Sound judgment characterized all of his decisions and he proved a most valuable worker in the efforts to form a practical organization. When the south was asked to name a member for the Board of Trustees, all eyes turned upon Mr. Colby who was elected without one dissenting vote. During that convention his anxiety and hard labor told upon his physical strength. He took cold and could not throw it off hence the foundations for his present illness was laid in Chicago. From Chicago, he visited his early home in Minnesota where he gained nothing over his cold but rather lost ground. He went to Washington to attend the meeting of the Trustees of the National Association on November 1st when he was stricken with hemorrhages and almost carried over into Spirit life. He was most kindly cared for by Drs. J. A. and Mrs. Cora Bland at whose pleasant home he fortunately found shelter. They have nursed him back to life and kind nature is slowly giving back his strength. His convalescence is slow but will surely ultimate in restored health.

A few words more and this personal sketch of our noble Brother will be brought to a close. This long illness has deprived Brother Colby of his engagements to lecture for at least four months—October and November have already passed and December and January will pass before he will be able to do any speaking. What is the duty of the Spiritualists of the United States in this case especially those whose privilege it is to be in his particular friends? The people to whom he has ministered ought to have found answers in their own hearts before reaching this particular question. Their duty is as clear as the sun at noonday and they will be remiss indeed in their conception of the ordinary business and sympathy if they fail in this instance to do justice to a true and tried worker, their friend and brother George P. Colby. No man has done more for Spiritualism in 30 years than has Geo. P. Colby; few have done as much and now it is come a time for the Spiritualists to prove their gratitude for his labors and to show that unlike Republican Spiritualism is grateful to all its heroes and honor them with a practical as well as affectionate remembrance. Let us honor ourselves in honoring this gifted, unselfish worker and fill the house of his enforced illness with the sunshine of love expressed in a way that he cannot fail to understand it.

Mr. Colby will remain at 1121 Tenth Street N. W. Washington, D.C. for sometime yet until he is able to endure the fatigue of a trip to Florida."

/s/ H. D. Barrett, 1893

Appendix B

Tribute and Memorial to Robert Bos and Mae Graves-Ward

A TRIBUTE AND MEMORIAL

There are two very special people who guided and enabled me to witness Mental Mediumship and the very best of Physical Mediumship within the gates of Cassadaga Spiritualist Camp. They freely offered their guidance for my unfoldment. I am blessed for having had the opportunity of having them in my life. In their honor, after their Memorial Service, I planted two cypress seedlings—one on each side of the Gazebo in Seneca Park. Their strength and outreach in height and width reflects the love and lives of Mama Mae and Robert.

ROBERT BOS

Robert, owner of the Joroco Motel in Daytona Beach, Florida was born on October 30, 1923 in New York. At the age of three he began to demonstrate an outstanding mediumistic and psychic ability. Although mediumistic, he never read for payment. It took a lot of convincing and finally in the early 1960s, he opened his office serving as a Medium in a rental apartment in Cassadaga Camp on the ground floor of 455 Seneca Street, Cassadaga.

His unfaltering guide, Thundercloud, made Robert world famous. Robert became known as Arthur Ford's medium. Robert traveled to Europe three months each year where he had regularly scheduled appointments with the Queen of England, the Queen of Holland, the President and others of Russian Government, and other dignitaries.

Having been as close as family and a true friend, he was my "encourager." We shared the platform in the Colby Auditorium many times in the late 1960s—I, as the orator, and he demonstrating Mediumship that surpassed all others. Without prior notice, Robert introduced me as the Medium of the Day in the Colby Auditorium.

Robert Bos made his transition on June 1, 1971. As he requested, his physical remains were interred at the bend in the road just below the chimes in the Bellevue Cemetery in Daytona Beach, Florida.

ROBERT BOS

MAE GRAVES-WARD

Rubella (aka Mae) Graves was born on November 15, 1905 in Potomac, Illinois and raised in Gary, Indiana. The "one and only" — there shall never be another just quite like her! Momma Mae was small in stature but large in her demonstration of Mediumship. Her joyful spirit gained her the title of the *Sophie Tucker of Spiritualism*. Mae served Spiritualism as an orator and medium and traveled to all parts of the United States serving Spiritualist Churches, Conventions and Camps.

Mae was blessed to have a philosophical side of her being and fortunate when Dr. Leland, a co-founder of Rutgers University identified himself as one of her guides. The response to a letter written to the University in 1984 confirmed the information Dr. Leland had given her during daily meditation many years earlier.

Mae resided with her husband, Sam at 1284 Stevens Street in the Cassadaga Spiritualist Camp diagonal from my residence at 447 Lake Street.

Since my mother graduated to the Higher Life in my younger years and Mae's daughter in the year of my birth, we adopted each other. Our day outings to Daytona included a nice lunch and a "shop till you drop" excursion filled with lots of laughter.

I was privileged to have my Ordination Service performed by Rev. Harrison Engle in the Colby Auditorium on June 3, 1973 chaired by Gladys Reid, Healer and Mae Graves-Ward administering the Oath of Ordination.

Mae Graves-Ward made her transition to the higher side of life on December 19, 1988 (my Mother's birthday). Her son Randy Clausen fulfilled her wish and saw that her physical remains were cremated.

MAE GRAVES-WARD

Appendix C

Guide for a Successful Reading

by The Rev. Wilbur Hull

1. RELAX. Seek a Medium's help at a time when you are relaxed and undisturbed. Put your mind at ease.

2. PATIENCE. Allow the Medium to proceed in his or her manner. Do not expect your problem to be discussed at once.

3. BE FAIR. No Medium wants or needs help, but do not attempt to confuse them. Let them know when they are correct.

4. EXPECT GOOD. Excessive skepticism, demanding proof, arguing or wanting things done your way only leads to failure.

5. WELCOME SPIRIT. Do not be too quick to say "no." Welcome the Spirit even if you are unable to recognize it immediately. Some messages may require time to be fully understood.

6. BE WILLING TO VERIFY. Spirit often manifests by name. Evidence comes in many other ways: description, relationship and simple tests.

7. GUIDANCE. The true value of a reading is not always measured by prophecy. Prediction is always possible, but you have free will to make changes. The key note is guidance.

8. EXPECT TRUTH. Mediumship is not fortune-telling. A good reading should explain the philosophy of right living and bring us to a better understanding of our potentials.

9. LENGTH OF SESSION. Do not try to prolong a reading. The Medium realizes when the force is gone.

10. EVERY MEDIUM has his or her unique way. It is unfair to compare the ability of Mediums.

11. INVITE SPIRIT. By going to a meeting where there is communication with the Spirit World, whether it be by means of a Circle, Public Séance, Outdoor

meeting or Private sitting, ask your Spirit loved ones to attend the meeting with you.

12. QUESTIONS. If you wish to ask questions, you should ask the Spirits well in advance of the meeting. Give them ample time to get an answer. No Spirit claims to have an answer on the spur of the moment.

13. REMEMBER. Although those in the Spirit World can see farther than we, they do not profess to have all the answers, just as we here in the physical world cannot know everything.

Appendix D

Original Declaration of Principles

Adopted

Principle 1-6 Chicago, Illinois—1899
Principle 7-8 Rochester, New York—1909
Principle 9 St. Louis Missouri—1944

Many organizations have used these principles as a guideline in developing principles to suffice their needs.

1. We believe in Infinite Intelligence.

2. We believe that the phenomena of nature, both physical and spiritual are the expression of Infinite Intelligence.

3. We affirm that a correct understanding of such expression and living in accordance therewith constitute true religion.

4. We affirm that the existence and personal identity of the individual continue after the change called death.

5. We affirm that communication with the so-called dead is a fact scientifically proven by the phenomena of Spiritualism.

6. We believe that the highest morality is contained in the Golden Rule: Whatsoever ye would that others should do unto you, do ye also unto them.

7. We affirm the moral responsibility of the individual, and that he makes his own happiness or unhappiness as he obeys or disobeys Nature's psychic and spiritual laws.

8. We affirm that the doorway to reformation is never closed against any human soul, here or hereafter.

9. We affirm that the precepts of Prophecy contained in the Bible are Divine attributes proven through Mediumship.

Appendix E

21st Century Affirmations & Explanation Of Progressive Spiritualists

I.

We affirm an Infinite Spirit.

Spiritualism expresses a belief in a higher source. After many years of proof, it is appropriate to replace the word 'believe' with 'affirm.'

II.

We affirm that the phenomena of nature both Spiritual and Physical are expressions of the Infinite Spirit.

Spiritualism has expressed its belief in the phenomena of nature for over 115 years; therefore the word 'believe' can be replaced with 'affirm.'

III.

**We affirm continued existence and personal
identity of the individual continue after
the soul discards the physical body.**

*The continuity of life with those who have discarded
the physical shell and now reside in the Spirit
World has been proven through mediumship.*

IV.

**We affirm that under proper conditions,
communication with those in the unseen spheres
is proven by the phenomena of Spiritualism.**

*The demonstration of mediumship has proven beyond
a doubt that we communicate with those who have
moved to the higher expression of a continuity of life.*

V.

**We affirm our personal responsibility;
our happiness or unhappiness depends
upon the choices we make.**

*The Law of Cause and effect clarifies that
our choice is the Cause and the Effect is the
result. We receive back what we put out.*

VI.

**We affirm the doorway of reformation is always
open to any human soul here or hereafter.**

Remove the negative term and replace with positive (open), the human mind is the only mind that allows for discernment.

VII.
We affirm the highest morality is expressed in the Golden Rule.
Most religions of the world teach and practice the Golden Rule.

VIII
We affirm that a correct understanding of the Natural Laws and living in accordance therewith constitute our understanding of true religion.
When we understand and live by the law, we are then living a true religion.

Appendix F

Contacts in Cassadaga

Brighid's Well

http://www.cassadagabrighidswell.com/

https://www.facebook.com/universalcentre.cassadaga

460 Cassadaga Road

407-246-8610 or 8586

Cassadaga Hotel

www.cassadagahotel.net/

https://www.facebook.com/pages/

Cassadaga-Hotel/155081811172796

355 Cassadaga Road

386-228-2323

Cassadaga Psychic Therapy Center

1048 W/S Marion Street

904-228-0389

Purple Rose
www.cassadaga-purplerose.com
https://www.facebook.com/pr1079?filter=2
1079 Stevens Street
386-228-3315

Sinatra's L'Aldila Restaurant/Cafe
In the Historic Cassadaga Hotel
www.sinatras.us
https://www.facebook.com/SinatrasRistorante
355 Cassadaga Road
386-218-3806

Southern Cassadaga Spiritualist Camp Meeting Association 'The Cassadaga Camp'
www.cassadaga.org/
https://www.facebook.com/cassadagaspiritualistcamp
112 Stevens Street
Bookstore & Welcoming Center
Book Store 386-228-2880 – Office 228-3171

RESEARCHED REFERENCES

A Pictorial History of West Volusia County, 1870-1940
Articles—Handwritten Oct. 26, 1896—SCSCMA
Beyond the Valley, 1885—Andrew Jackson Davis
Boston News Journal, 1904—Sam Hayden
Buffalo Evening News, Sep 1982—The Other Cassadaga
Colby Family History—provided by Colby's family descendant
Corinthian Hall Magazine, 1849
Deland Sun News, Dec. 28-29, 1985 & 1949
De Leon Springs Courier, 1886.
Events in the Life of a Seer, 1848—Andrew Jackson Davis
History of Fillmore County, The Tale of Cherry Grove, 1984
Hydesville in History, 1917—M. E. Cadwallader
King James Bible
Life Work of Mrs. Cora L. V. Richmond, 1895—H. D. Barrett
Magazines, Selected 1852-2000
Manuals NSA 1920-1952 & NSAC 1953-2004
Marion Skidmore Library, Lily Dale, N.Y.—Selected Files
Minutes, 1859—National Spiritualist Association
Minutes of 1st Formative Convention, 1893—Bound, NSA
Museum, Lily Dale, N.Y.—Selected Files and Magazines
NSA Archives—Selected Files
Path of Light, Volume I & II, 2014—Marilyn J. Awtry
Personal Correspondence between John Drummond, Caretaker of
    the Hydesville Cottage and Marilyn J. Awtry
Psychic Observer, Editor, Ralph Pressings—Selected issues.
River of Life—How to Live in the Flow, 2007—Marilyn J. Awtry
Southern Cassadaga Spiritualist Camp Meeting Association
    (Selected flyers, booklets, letters)
Story of Deland and Lake Helen by Helen Deland, FL, 1909 E. O.
    Painter, Printer
The Missing Link, Reprint, 1965—L. Underhill, Thomas & Knox
    Co., N.Y.
The Progressive Thinker, Various Issues—Ed. M. E. Cadwallader
The National Spiritualist-Summit—Selected Issues

The New Educational Course on Modern Spiritualism, 1983,
  MPI—Marilyn J. Awtry and Paula Vogt
The Sunflower, 1985, MPI—Marilyn J. Awtry
Unwilling Martyrs, 1947—M. B. Pond—Spiritual News Pub.
Volusia County Courthouse Records, 1873-1986
Who's Who in Spiritualism of Yesteryear—Pioneers of Modern
  Spiritualism Vol. 1 & 2—Marilyn J. Awtry, S.A.M. Inc. 1980

Marilyn J. Awtry
Authored

Booklets
The Symbol of Spiritualism, 1975
You and a Way (5th Reprint), 1977
Around the World to Bicentennial Spiritualism, 1977
Books, Books, and More Books on Spiritualism, 1977
Introductory Approach to Natural Law, 1977
Pioneers of Spiritualism, 1977
Understanding the Philosophy of A. J. Davis, 1977
A Study in Mediumship and Phenomena, 1978
The Philosophy of Spiritualism, 1979
Who's Who in Spiritualism—Vol. I & II, 1979
Brighten Your Way—A Daily Devotional, 1983
The History of the NSAC, 1983
They Paved the Way, 2000

Courses & Seminars
A Psychic You—The Big Picture
Dreams and the Spirit Connection
Mediumship Energetics
New Educational Course on Modern Spiritualism
Stepping Stones of Spiritualism
Tapping Your Ultimate Skills
The Intuitive You
The Rhythmic Universe
Spirit Photography at Its Best
You Can Have it All

Columnist
Psychic World (UK) & The National Spiritualist (NSAC)

Spiritualism & More (SAM, INC.*)

Natural Law Governs Study & Work Book, 1979

A Poet Ponders, 1979

Psychic Puzzler No. 1, 1979

A Spiritualist View of the Bible, 1981

Contemporary Definitions of Psychic Phenomena and Related
Subjects, 1980

Booklets Reprinted/Pub by SAM Inc.

A Lecture on Spiritualism by Dr. Geo. B. Warne

Clairvoyance and How to do Good

Hermione—A Psychic Study, Cora Richmond

The Law of Suggestion, W. J. Colville

Premier of Modern Spiritualism, William Elliott Hammond

Origin of Modern Spiritualism—Hydesville Cottage, M. E.
Cadwallader

Universal Ethical Teachings, Their Source, Value and Law of
Suggestion by W. J. Colville

Calendar

Spiritualism Millennium Calendar, 2000

*SAM = Spiritualism & More—Marilyn Awtry & Paula Vogt

Web: www.marilynjawtry.com

About The Author

MARILYN J. AWTRY

Marilyn has been a Spiritualist for more than 50 years. She has become known as "The Walking Encyclopedia of Spiritualism of the 21st Century." She is well-known as a National Teacher, Orator and Spirit Intermediary.

As an author/journalist, she has served on the TNS Staff—Contributing Editor 1978-1979 and as columnist for 49 years; commissioned by the M.P.I. to co-author "The New Educational Course on Modern Spiritualism," 1979; Editor of *The Cassadagan,* Cassadaga, Florida 1988-1989; Editor of *Speakout,* monthly publication of the Harmonial Philosophy Association, 1987-1990; USA Correspondent for the *Psychic World* of England, 2009-current.

Marilyn was appointed by the NSAC Board of Directors as a Trustee in 1984. She was elected by the Delegates of the 91st Annual Convention for another three-year term. Nominated again in 1987, she declined the nomination. In 1992, she was featured in a story about Spiritualism and the Southern Cassadaga Spiritualist Campmeeting Association on the Maury Povich Show.

Marilyn is recognized in Who's Who of American Women, 1983—Women of the World, 1984—Cambridge's Who's Who 2011—Worldwide Publishing 17th Edition, 2013.

Website: www.marilynjawtry.com
Email: Spiritraps@aol.com
Don't miss the monthly updates of
"Thoughts to Ponder" and "Sunflower Seeds".

CPSIA information can be obtained
at www.ICGtesting.com
Printed in the USA
BVHW071704090620
581035BV00002B/100